DANGEROUS
CUSTOMER SERVICE

DANGEROUS CUSTOMER SERVICE

Dangerously Great Customer Service...How to Achieve it and Maintain it

Impact Innovation

Phil Davis and Kate Stenner

BLOOMSBURY

First published in Great Britain 2011

Bloomsbury Publishing Plc
50 Bedford Square
London WC1B 3DP

A CIP record for this book is available from the British Library.

ISBN: 978-1-4081-2502-1

This book is produced using paper that is made from wood grown in managed, sustainable forests. It is natural, renewable and recyclable. The logging and manufacturing processes conform to the environmental regulations of the country of origin.

Design by Fiona Pike, Pike Design, Winchester
Typeset by Saxon Graphics, Derby
Printed and bound by CPI Group UK Ltd, Croydon, CR0 4YY

CONTENTS

ACKNOWLEDGEMENTS

The authors would like to thank the following members of the Impact Innovation team for their support, guidance and ideas: Simon Gardner, Nick Fawcett, Sharron Fenemore, Charlotte Leyland, Kim Ellwood, and Monica Chauhan.

And to thank all of our wonderful clients who have trusted us to help improve their customer service and from whom we have learnt so much.

introduction

Dangerous, what do you mean dangerous? What could be so dangerous about this innocent-looking book, you'll be wondering. And it's true – you're not in any danger of it biting your hand off or running amok and wrecking your office. However, it is dangerous in a number of other senses:

- It contains very little theory, very little management language, very little academic gloss. We haven't done huge amounts of research into different organisations, or read vast quantities of the latest business thinking. It is clothed in very little, you might believe, *except* (and this is a big except) our own experience and the experience of our clients. In other words, it is standing here naked apart from its underclothes. But as you'll see from all the masses of practical stories and examples we've included, those underclothes are woven from reality – so it is not embarrassed about flaunting itself!
- The book is written in a very chatty, talkative style. You might hate it. But we wanted to write as if we were talking to you, not preaching or compiling an academic thesis.
- Some of it challenges conventional thinking on customer service. There's a big danger that you won't agree with us. That's OK – as long as it provokes you to do some thinking yourself.
- Speaking of challenges, this book constantly challenges *you* to go and do something to improve the experience your customers get from you. It also dares you to do things you might not have done before. Dangerous? Well, at least *adventurous*, in this instance.
- We've made a lot of assumptions about what you already know and what you can do. So we haven't gone into the minutiae of telling you how to heat the water before you can have boiled eggs for breakfast. That would have resulted in an enormous, and much less interesting, book. Is it dangerous to assume that you're an intelligent reader? You decide!

So who are we to go writing dangerous books on customer service – especially when it's the first in a series of dangerous business management books?

Maybe our client list should do the talking. We've worked with Tesco, Accor, Eurostar, O2, Waitrose, John Lewis and plenty more. Many of our customers have won awards for the work they've done in customer service. *We've* won awards for the work we've done with our customers in their work in customer service (untangle that one if you can!). In recent days we've been working extensively with the NHS to improve their patient experience, and as a result, we've developed a number of approaches, thoughts and ideas – tried and tested in real situations – over the last 10 years that we feel are worth sharing.

We hope you agree. We hope that you enjoy this book. We hope that even if you don't, you'll find some nuggets here and there that will inspire you in your own business dealings. Apart from anything else, your customers deserve it – and you will have a lot more fun.

All the very best of luck to you!

The Impact team

chapter 1
emotional, rational and lifetime loyalty

oyalty cards; loyalty schemes; loyalty bonuses; loyalty points; loyalty discounts. The 'L' word is everywhere these days, and all businesses are chasing it madly. There are three great reasons for doing so: if customers are loyal, they come back to you over and over again; they say nice things about you to their friends and contacts, and they spend more money with you per transaction than they would otherwise. In other words, loyalty gains you three extra revenue streams *on top* of your core business earnings. So you could say that the ultimate goal of any business is to create and maintain loyalty among the people who purchase your goods and services.

However, there's some confusion about what we mean by the word loyalty. All those cards/schemes/bonuses etc. don't actually have anything to do with loyalty at all. They are to do with rewards. Would you describe yourself as loyal if you go to a particular bank purely because there's something in it for you? No. If a different bank offered you something even more beneficial, you'd go there instead.

So what is loyalty then?

The Oxford Concise English Dictionary definition of the word loyal is 'steadfast in allegiance', and there are two main types of loyalty:

Rational loyalty – This is all based on 'head' decisions. People are faithful to a particular supplier because it gives them exactly what they want or need.

Emotional loyalty – The heart makes the choices. Customers really care about a supplier, for all kinds of different reasons, and have an emotional investment in their purchases.

In addition to these there is **lifetime loyalty**, a special case of emotional loyalty which we discuss at the end of this chapter, and **staff loyalty**, which is so important we've devoted a whole chapter to it later in the book.

SO WHAT SHOULD YOU AIM AT - HEAD OR HEART?
Head
Rational loyalty is vital. If you don't give your customers what they need, you've had it, end of story. Most first-time purchases are made for rational reasons. People shop at supermarkets that are near them; they go to restaurants that they've been told about by friends; they go to specialist shops because those are the only places that stock 1 inch Wonkywidgets X14NY; they buy flights from easyJet because they're cheap. All are rational choices. Even brand-based purchases are made largely for rational reasons, although this varies somewhat according to industry sector. Brands in clothing, for example, have an element of emotional appeal in that they tend to mean something specific to customers. However, people don't generally buy goods from Poundstretcher because they're big fans of the brand – they buy them because they know Poundstretcher is cheap, just as most wouldn't wear a T-shirt with 'I shop at Tesco' proudly emblazoned across their chests.

It's quite easy to improve rational loyalty. You can repaint all your stores to look more fashionable; you can introduce a new line of yoghurts for mums-to-be or the latest 'it' product; you can cut the price of your cheap flights even further. But the trouble is, if it's not difficult for you to make these improvements, it's not difficult for your competitors to do the same. All appeals to your customers' rational faculties are quite simple to copy, and that leaves you vulnerable.

Heart
Emotional loyalty, on the other hand, has a power of its own. Customers invest of themselves in certain providers, for a variety of reasons. This can be anything from loving the relaxing

dangerous customer service

atmosphere of a restaurant to approving of a company's ethical stance – like The Body Shop, for example. Two of our staff members are intensely loyal to their village shop, one because the owner is charming and delightful to her and her family; the other because he believes passionately that small local businesses must be supported or they'll disappear. In the first instance, the emotional 'hook' is service that makes her feel cared for; in the second, it's a principle.

From a supplier's point of view, there are two great advantages in emotional loyalty. Firstly, customers will forgive you at least one mistake and, moreover, they'll feel guilty if they leave. A friend we know, for example, put up with awful haircuts for years because the hairdresser was such a nice guy. After one bodge too many, though, even she felt she had to go elsewhere – but she couldn't bear to go to another hairdresser in the same salon. It had to be somewhere completely different, where she wouldn't be in danger of meeting him and having to explain. Secondly, emotional loyalty enables you to push your pricing further than you could otherwise do so. This is borne out by Fairtrade products, for instance. You can charge a lot more for Fairtrade bananas than for unidentified ones and sell just as many. People like to know that the grower's being properly paid for his or her labours.

Of the two types of loyalty, then, emotional has much the greatest power.

pause for thought...

It's difficult to measure emotional loyalty, but the 'drive by' test is a good one to reflect on. How many similar suppliers would a customer be prepared to drive past in order to arrive at your front door? If the answer is 'none', you've got work to do!

exercise

WHAT'S IN YOUR WALLET?

Wherever you are now, find your wallet/purse/handbag and take out your store cards/credit cards/bank cards/car keys/mobile phone/whatever. Think carefully about what each one means to you. Do you feel loyal to the provider? If so, is your loyalty rational or emotional? Bank cards are nearly always rational. National Trust cards are nearly always emotional. Store cards are often called loyalty cards, but they're not really. You might find you've got a Tesco one, a Sainsbury's one *and* a Somerfield one. Do they indicate your loyalty? No – they're a means of getting something that benefits you (points, bonuses, rewards etc). Which mobile phone do you use? What car do you drive? Why?

CAN YOU RUN A BUSINESS ON ONE TYPE OF LOYALTY ALONE?

The short answer to this is yes. But it's a qualified yes, partly dependent on sector. Quite a few businesses run on rational loyalty alone, providing their customers with what they want or need but no more – Ryanair, for instance. Petrol stations can keep going, as long as they have fuel; monopolies can keep going, as long as no competitors enter the market. We think, though, that the only reason any business can function on rational loyalty alone is the current poor state of the customer experience. There are opportunities in almost any sector to steal a march on the competition by improving emotional loyalty.

So all the focus for businesses should be on gaining emotional loyalty? But by itself, this isn't enough either – and concentrating on it too much can be detrimental. For instance, in spite of huge spend on luscious adverts that plucked the heartstrings and taste buds, Marks & Spencer experienced disastrous food sales over Christmas. Why is not immediately apparent, but it could be the fact that many of M&S's biggest stores are on high streets, rather than in big out-of-town retail parks which really pull in the Christmas crowds. So rational convenience, in this case, might well have trumped emotional appeal. In any case it's certainly possible to stretch a customer's emotional loyalty too far. M&S also had serious problems with their online business at Christmas. Orders poured in, but there was so much upset caused by goods arriving on the wrong day/not at all/being out of stock that it made the national press. Many charities made the same mistake, proving that all the goodwill in the world cannot offset faulty delivery and fulfilment systems. As Sandi Toksvig, writing in the *Sunday Telegraph*, asked wryly, 'Just how cross are you allowed to be, if you've ordered from a charity and it doesn't turn up?'

ALTERING THE BALANCE

So, we've established that:

1. Without your customers' rational loyalty, you're dead in the water.

2. Whatever your business, you can improve both your own position and your competitive edge by earning the emotional loyalty of your customers.

You need both, in other words.

And this is where creating the right customer service experience has its big opportunity. As we said before, nearly all first purchases are made for rational reasons. But once that choice is made you can use the customer service experience to 1) fulfil rational expectations and 2) to deliver an element of emotional experience. The latter has the power to change customers' thinking slightly so that decision-making the second time around might be more of a balance – rational AND emotional.

Budget hotels are a great example. Almost everyone chooses them on a) location and b) price, and it's pot luck which brand they pick – Ibis, Travelodge, Premier Inn etc. But by introducing a great customer service experience, you can change the way they select in future and what they tell their friends (i.e. great experience, go there). In other words, you gain repeat or referral – two of the additional revenue streams that result from loyalty. In future, the decision-making process might be a) location and b) is there an Ibis near there?, c) let's look on the website...*now you've got them*. But if you don't deliver the emotional experience, you'll never change their decision-making process.

pause for thought...

Loyalty does not just apply to premium brands. People always think if you're paying more, you can have extra customer service and all the little frills that make something seem special. Not true – it's just as important for budget brands. Anyone can create a great experience, regardless of what the business or product is, and whether it's high or low price.

THE EFFECT OF CUSTOMER SERVICE ON LOYALTY

Providing a great customer experience is what this book's all about, and we'll be examining many different aspects in the following chapters, but there is one essential principle that lies at the heart of everything else. This is best illustrated by looking at the case of regular customers, those people who come back and buy from you again and again. Say you run a budget hotel. Your regulars, although they're valuable to you and you regard them as special, are, after all, just customers. They purchase exactly the same product as all other customers – same drinks in the bar, same rooms, same everything. The difference lies in the experience they receive.

When we were doing work for one well-known hotel chain, we discovered that regulars and one-off (or new) customers tend to experience extraordinarily different levels of service. We saw the same member of staff, in the space of a few minutes, greet one customer with joyful recognition and warm enquiries about his family and journey, and the next with a polite, but cool, 'Yes? Do you have a reservation sir?' This is all very nice for the first customer, but what about the second? He too is a customer, but now he feels like a second-class one.

This becomes even more interesting when you compare the experiences of different regulars. Most of those we spoke to adored the hotel, the staff, the service and couldn't speak highly enough of them. One man, however, was pretty so-so about the service he received. 'It's OK' was the best he could manage, and he was a real regular among regulars, having stayed in the hotel once a month every month for the past two years. On this particular visit, he'd exchanged precisely two words with members of the hotel staff – one 'hello' in the lift, and one at reception. So why was this? It happens that this gentleman was not particularly forthcoming. He wasn't unpleasant in any way, just not very proactive in initiating conversation, and this led us to a very important question:

Are you nice to your regulars because you value them as regulars, or is it because *they are nice to you and your staff?*

In other words, that warm friendly relationship you have with some customers that you're so proud of...is it in fact initiated by the customers themselves, and not by you? Think about it.

If you come to the same conclusion as us – that some customers *attract* wonderful service and others do not – you'll also realise that it's a simple problem to fix. In fact it's so easy, a machine can do it. Many of the companies rated best for customer service are Internet businesses, which have no face-to-face interaction at all. The pinnacle of these is Amazon, the online retailer. If you've ever bought, say, a book from them before, you're greeted by name when you log on to their site; you're given lists of other books you might like, based on your previous purchases; you're asked if you want goods despatched to your usual address or a different one, and so on. Machines have certain advantages over their human counterparts in this sort of instance, being capable of storing vast databases of names, addresses, purchase histories etc., but this is largely irrelevant. The real point here is that the most successful service providers **take the initiative**. *They* make all the moves to begin the relationship-building process with customers. Whether customers choose to respond is then up to them – but the way is clear for both sides to embrace each other and the first seeds of loyalty are sown.

This is good news for you and your business. All you need to do to make dramatic improvements in your customer relationships is to learn – and to teach your staff – to **be brave** and take the first steps. Smile, look people in the eye, say hello or remark on the weather...anything really, as long as it's obviously benign. Staff have a far more powerful potential to create a relationship than a machine does. So if you have staff, you have the potential to use their power, whatever your business. It's a big opportunity for almost any organisation.

pause for thought...

Around 10 per cent of staff are naturally great service providers and will take the initiative. The majority (80 per cent) are not and react to how customers are with them. However, when asked, they think that the relationship is all to do with them and that they have created it. Wrong. The remaining 10 per cent may find making any kind of relationship with a customer difficult – they may be good at customer transactions but not good at customer service!

PROVING THE POINT

Can it really be this easy? And does it truly make a difference to your bottom line? Well yes, actually – to both questions.

We helped Tesco to introduce their 'Living Service', a campaign across all stores helping staff to be proactive, warm and friendly in the service they provided to customers. The results were fantastic. Like for like, 'Living Service' stores outperformed non-'Living Service' stores by 20 per cent, not just in sales but with an additional increase in staff morale, staff friendliness and levels of management support.

dangerous challenge

'LET'S GET EMOTIONAL WITH OUR CUSTOMERS'

You and your staff proactively take the initiative with as many of your customers as possible. Customers buying things – tell them what a great choice that is. Customers with children – tell them how great their children are. Customers with unusual ties – tell them how great their tie is. Phone your non-regular customers and ask them for feedback (not more sales). If your customers are businesses, phone them and tell them how brilliant their latest advert/product/whatever is. Spend at least one day proactively engaging with your customers in an emotional way.

THE TIME YOU TAKE

Spending time with a customer isn't actually the same as delivering service to that customer, but it will do as a measure for now. Think about your different types of customer and how much time you spend with each, typically it divides roughly like this: (marketeers may well be in shock with this rough and ready segmentation but please forgive us).

Customer type	Proportion of your customer base	Time you spend at each transaction
Doris – the super-friendly chatter.	5 per cent	2 mins
Arthur – always something to complain about.	1 per cent	10 mins
All the rest of your customers – nice, open, quite friendly people, happy to chat if spoken to.	94 per cent	2 seconds – hello, thank you, good bye, if you're lucky.

Now think about whether this is the best use of your time?

Doris's customer type – They already love you – so of course be nice to them, but be careful not to spend too long doing it.

Arthur's customer type – We're talking about the sort of customers who are *never* going to be happy. Do you actually want them? Is it really worth spending such a big proportion of your time on them? The customer is *not* always right, shock horror. But do note that people with a genuine problem or complaint are in a completely different class...you have the opportunity with them to start creating lifetime loyalty (see opposite), so it's vital to make sure you resolve their complaints properly.

All the rest of your customers – Spending such a relatively small proportion of your time on the vast majority of your customers means that you're missing important opportunities. You could be converting at least another 5 per cent to regulars or ambassadors.

DON'T LET THE BAD DICTATE THE SERVICE YOU GIVE TO THE GOOD...OR THE UGLY (WE CAN'T ALL BE BEAUTIFUL)

We all know there are a few people out there who can take advantage and try to get something for nothing. We have all heard them...'No I haven't worn the dress, I just don't like it now...'; 'No, I didn't watch the pay TV in my room last night...'. But why do we design our service experience to stop these very, very few customers from taking advantage? I know companies don't want people to take advantage of them, but why should we all be treated as if we are dishonest?

At breakfast in a hotel 'Can I have your room number?' seems to be asked so that people who haven't booked breakfast can't get breakfast for free. Where is the 'Welcome to breakfast, did you sleep well? What is your name? Mr Davis, I hope you enjoy a great breakfast' then?

dangerous challenge

HAVE A 'WE TRUST EVERYONE DAY'

Change your processes and your attitude to everyone and act as if you trust us all – see what happens.

LIFETIME LOYALTY

Lifetime loyalty is a special case – the most intense – of emotional loyalty. As such, it's something that many companies set as their end objective, the thing they most want to encourage in their customers. We don't think, though, that it's a realistic aim. Lifetime loyalty almost always arises out of crisis, and you obviously can't go round creating crises for your customers! However, it's important to understand why and when lifetime loyalty arises, so that you can learn to seize the opportunities if they do come along.

13

The deepest lifetime loyalty emerges from the deepest crises. The best example we've found is the man who simply won't hire a car unless it's from Alamo. He even chooses the airports he flies into based on whether or not Alamo operates out of there. This is because of an event in his childhood. At the age of 12, he became very ill on a family holiday to America and it was uncertain when he would be well enough to fly home; it was a very stressful situation for the whole family. It also meant that every fortnight for the next three months his Dad had to renew the car hire. When he finally got better, the family went to settle the Alamo bill – but the manager, who knew their circumstances, refused to take any payment whatsoever. He said it was the least he could do. From that day on, no other car company had the slightest chance of renting a vehicle to any member of that family.

Obviously not all problems are this severe, but almost everyone has an emotional response when something goes wrong, even if it's only minor. For example, say you buy something and then decide you don't want it after all. You'll probably experience a low level of anxiety, as you're never quite sure what reaction you'll get from the supplier. So there's actually more emotional investment in taking the item back than there was in purchasing it in the first place. Understanding this in how they respond is the way suppliers begin to build lifetime loyalty. This is one reason why M&S gained so much lifetime loyalty in the early days. At the time, returning items wasn't really done and few shops allowed it without a fuss. But M&S stumbled on it...you didn't need your receipt and you might even have worn the item, but they'd take it back with no questions asked. Amazing! Everyone loved them. They'd anticipated the emotional issue.

So creating lifetime loyalty is all about spotting and understanding the level of crisis and providing resolution. But be warned: this also works in reverse. Generally speaking, the problem itself is often not the problem. The problem is what arises if an issue is poorly handled. For a customer, it's not necessarily a big deal if they are given a smoking room by mistake when they have specifically requested a non-smoking one. But if they are then told that, no, they cannot be moved...then a big row, very cross customer and awkward problem are likely the results!

exercise

FINDING THE FLAWS

It's worth thinking about the fact that some types of crisis vary from generation to generation. The AA and RAC, for example, enjoyed fanatical devotion from their customers for years, due to the fact that cars weren't very reliable. People rescued at the roadside tend to be immensely grateful. Nowadays, however, breakdowns are less frequent and rescue companies have to work harder to gain business and retain loyalty. Are there examples of typical modern problems facing your customers that you could be better geared up to resolve? It could be well worth your while.

key learning points

- Most 'loyalty' schemes are not about loyalty, they're about rewards, which is a different thing. Don't spend too much money on them.
- To be really successful, you need to earn both rational and emotional loyalty from your customers.
- Providing great customer service is the best way to build powerful emotional loyalty.
- Good customer relationships are often (too often) generated by the customer and not you, whatever you might think.

- Taking the initiative with customers, even in simple ways, can make an enormous difference to your bottom line.
- Gaining lifetime loyalty is a case of learning to seize opportunities when they arise. It's unrealistic to set it as an overall objective.

chapter 2
basics and magic

In Chapter 1 we have established that in order to succeed in business you need your customers' loyalty – both rational and emotional – and that you use customer service and the customer experience to secure that loyalty.

So now you need to think about what the customer experience actually consists of?

We think it boils down into two parts: the basics and the magic.

Basics – are the things customers simply *expect* from your business or service – clean plates and glasses in a restaurant; the ability to access their money quickly and easily from a bank; helpful, speedy service at the supermarket checkout.

Magic – means the little unexpected extras that transform the customer experience into one of delight – the complimentary birthday drink; the surprise upgrade to business class on a flight.

Unsurprisingly, it's the 'magic' bits that people talk about when recounting experiences of great customer service. These are what stick in the mind. So, equally unsurprisingly, companies spend a great deal of time and money pursuing the magic, looking for the special little extras that will make their customers appreciate them. They think that it's magic that will help them gain more customer loyalty and therefore increase revenue – so why spend too much time on anything else?

But **stop right there**.

There is one thing that customers talk about even more than magic moments: the times when *basic* things aren't right. Rude staff, dirty hotels, late trains, the wrong goods – all are the stuff of legend. And what's more, people aren't content to tell only their friends and families about these things, they tell *everyone*.

LESSONS IN THE BASICS

So let's set magic aside for a minute and examine just how

essential basics are. We think there are three vital lessons to learn about basics.

1. Legendary service comes from getting the basics right

Consider this. ING Direct – the bank – has won a host of awards for customer service, and it does nothing magical at all. No frills, no furbelows, no one-off this or special offer that. What it does, though, is to do exactly what it says it will – every single time. In other words, it has thought very carefully about its basics and ensured it meets its customers' expectations, *without fail*. Very few companies do this. And customers are so pleased and delighted when they find it, they vote ING top of the service ratings every time.

John Lewis (voted the UK's best retailer) is another one. The company has earned this title through its relentless commitment to its basics. You are gently acknowledged by members of staff as you walk into each section of the store – not an in-your-face 'Can I help you?', but just a smile or a hello. This is surely a basic. The staff on each section know their products in detail – again, surely a basic. John Lewis is now the benchmark of customer service, not through magic but through its consistent delivery of the ordinary, everyday stuff.

In short, simply fulfilling the basics really well, without mistakes, every single time, is in itself a kind of magic.

2. Your basics are your brand

When companies think about their brand, they tend to think about everything that's best about their service/product/stores etc. – what's most modern or exciting or cutting edge. We're used to hearing Waitrose or M&S or some other big company saying things like, 'Our new flagship store that's just opened in X is the epitome of our brand...'. In other words, organisations look at the top end of what they deliver and think that is representative of their whole business. But this is an illusion – it's just not true.

The great majority of your customers won't be visiting your new food hall in the centre of Oxford. They'll be in your 20-year-old store on the outskirts of Crawley, or Milton Keynes, or Sheffield, or wherever. And their experience may be significantly different. So your brand is what your average customer experiences on an average day on an average week in your average outlet with your average member of staff. In fact, your brand is your bog standard! And don't just take our word for it – research has proved the point. One study showed that even with millions of pounds spent on advertising, sponsorship, celebrity endorsements, trendy new stores, swish logos etc., 80 per cent of the brand perception by customers was formed *in the last three feet*; in other words, at the moment of transaction. Whether it's online, in store or by your staff, this is the most important moment, when your brand lives or dies.

So we suggest that you make a copy of the following, blow it up as big as your printer will allow, and pin it to your wall:

> **Your brand is your basics, NOT your magic**
> **(especially when it comes to the customer**
> **experience or customer service)**

3. Proper investment in your basics is vital

Because of lessons 1) and 2), it is absolutely crucial to make sure you choose the right basics. This is for two reasons.

a. They must be right for your brand
    Think about how much time and money is spent on new corporate logos in order to make sure they reflect the right image of a company. Then compare this with the time spent in your organisation on deciding what the basics of your service experience are. We will eat our hats if the two bear any resemblance to one another. But this

is all the wrong way round – the service you offer to your customers reflects your brand just as much as, if not more than, your advertising, logos, stationery etc. Could it be time to re-prioritise?

b. They must be possible for your staff to deliver well every time

Let's consider Ryanair – an unlikely example to quote in a book on customer service so it would seem. But like it or loathe it, you have to admire the way its brand is so consistently delivered. Ryanair has a policy of no refunds once you have booked. A passenger phoned customer service, explaining that she had booked a flight for her mother, but her mother had just been killed in a car accident. Was it possible to have her money back? This woman was clearly very upset. Surely anyone would say that these were exceptional circumstances and of course they would provide a refund? Not Ryanair. It is the low-cost airline through and through; it has a clear policy and there are **no** exceptions. The answer was no.

What's the point of this story? Well, it may have been terrible customer service, but it is completely unmistakable to everyone what the Ryanair brand is all about. Staff are absolutely clear on what is expected of them **and** it is very consistent. Once you start making exceptions, it all becomes much more difficult and confusing and contradictory.

So, while you probably don't want to be like Ryanair, choose your basics, get them clear and stick to them...even if some of your customers don't like them. Maybe they shouldn't fly with Ryanair or buy from you!

Before you even think about adding magic, then, check your basics:

- What is your brand and how should it be expressed in the basics of your customer experience and service?
- What are the core standards that should be delivered in your organisation?
- Are they simple to understand, for everyone?
- Have you thought about both *what* happens and *how* it happens?
- Have you got these right?
- Are you sure?
- Are you really sure you're sure?
- Is your basic service consistent – the same for every customer, every day, without fail?

All the magic in the world will count for nothing if you don't deliver properly. Consider yourself warned.

pause for thought...

An episode in a recent series of 'The Apprentice' saw candidates setting up and running a laundry business. One team was particularly pleased with themselves for adding a 24-hour 'customer careline' to the service offered. At least they were until it was pointed out to them, in Sir Alan Sugar's characteristically blunt fashion, that a) customers were exceedingly unlikely to want to enquire after the welfare of their knickers in the middle of the night, and b) it sure as heck didn't help anything when punters all got the wrong clothes back the next morning!

ADDING THE MAGIC

Having said all this about basics, of course magic is important too – and of course you should look at ways of providing it in your service offering. The greatest customer service, which is what we're talking about, always brings with it the element of delight.

So, where to begin?

Let's start by thinking about the nature of magic. On first impressions, magic often looks spontaneous. For instance, you're 75 and buying wine, and the lady at the checkout peers smilingly over her glasses at you and says, 'Are you sure you're over 18, sir?' The hotel you're staying in has run out of vegetarian meals, so the receptionist dashes down to the local supermarket to buy more ingredients, just for you. And it's true to say that some of the very best stories about customer service involve a feeling of spontaneity for the customer.

However, there are two problems with spontaneity:

1. It is reactive. The magic only occurs when a particular situation is met with the perfect response. There's no element of proactivity at all.

2. It can't be relied upon. The right situation may not arise, or the person dealing with it might be having a bad day and respond grumpily instead. Result: no magic (or worse).

But there are other types of magic too, which are possible to conjure up deliberately.

Planned magic

One of the most astonishing 'little bits of magic' we've come across was when Charlotte, one of our colleagues, booked a hotel room. She got into a conversation with the receptionist on the phone and they got round to talking about children, Charlotte's nieces in particular. The receptionist had nieces the same age and said she'd love a photo of Charlotte's girls, so Charlotte sent her one. When Charlotte got to the hotel for her stay there, she found that photo, carefully framed, on her bedside table! Now that took some planning. The same goes for those restaurants which supply colouring books and crayons to keep children happy while the adults enjoy their meal. Such nice little bits and pieces don't just happen, they have to be chosen, purchased and kept stocked up – planned, in other words.

Another example can be taken from another hotel – a lovely old, historic place – when our colleague Simon checked in. He commented on how lovely the décor was and the receptionist said that, as he was interested, he would show him to his room and explain a little of the history on the way. What a great piece of spontaneous magic – or was it? Did it matter that when Simon was passing back through reception that evening, there was another guest having the history of the hotel explained to them whilst being shown to their room?

Planned magic that seems spontaneous

You might think that magic just happens, and only happens with certain types of people – your natural service givers – and you should simply be glad that it does. But this isn't really true. Creating the right climate for it to flourish in makes a huge difference.

For example, when we were working for Tesco, we looked at their 'SOS' guideline for checkout staff (**S**ay hello, **O**ffer help, **S**ay goodbye). Because a supermarket is a very process-driven business, some staff had interpreted this as another process that had to be followed and there they all were, SOS-ing away dutifully. But how boring was that...can you imagine, hundreds of customers every day, 'Hello', 'Can I help you', 'Goodbye'. The greatest communicator in the world simply couldn't fill that with sparkle and enthusiasm time after time. The poor staff needed some leeway – freedom to be a bit more like themselves. Very simply, the staff needed a little permission to vary what they could say and the managers needed to be able to trust staff to say appropriate things.

The big question for policy makers is always, 'But won't staff start doing all sorts of things and be too much out of control?'. Well what do you think? If you had permission to be yourself, would you go out of control? Trust your staff a little and they will reward you.

dangerous challenge

'UN-TRAIN' YOUR STAFF

Service processes can be very helpful, but they can also turn into straightjackets. How do you think a customer feels when a McDonald's operative says 'Have a nice day' to every customer every time? Try:

- rewarding initiative when staff do something unusual in the way of service;
- listening to them when they're with customers and publicly celebrating any outstanding examples of helpfulness or consideration;
- freeing them up from too many rules and regulations;
- not penalising those who bend rules, as long as it's in a constructive way;
- giving them the power to use their own discretion.

Do these regularly and you'll start to build a culture where magic can happen.

Breaking-the-rules magic

A particularly special kind of magic happens when customers feel that rules are being bent or broken in order to do them a favour. For instance, one of our colleagues bought a new set of bedroom furniture from MFI. It took weeks of evenings and weekends to put all the flat packs together and, typically, the very last box to be opened (the plinth round the bottom of the chest of drawers) turned out to be the wrong colour. It was well and truly outside the 72-hour 'check and exchange' time specified, so she rang MFI expecting to have to buy another plinth. But the fellow on the phone was extremely cheerful and nice. 'I'm in a good mood this morning,' he said. 'I'll pretend I don't know when you bought it and send you another. Don't tell anyone, will you!' She was thrilled, needless to say. But this couldn't have happened if the man hadn't been confident of his freedom to make such a decision.

pause for thought...

In one of Tesco's stores, we saw a woman who worked on the checkout desks with a little girl sitting on her lap helping to scan items through. The child was blind, and loved to be able to 'see' all the items with her fingers and help to 'beep' them through the till. She and her mum came every week and loved the whole experience. Other customers too smiled and were impressed whenever they saw this. But what about health and safety, or security?

Bearing in mind that the very words 'health and safety' are enough to send most customers climbing straight up the nearest wall, what do you think should have happened? Should the checkout lady have been reprimanded for rule infringement, or praised for her exceptional customer service skills? What would have happened if that member of staff had subsequently had to tell the little girl that she wasn't allowed to help any more?

Magic through humour

Another instant creator of spontaneous magic is humour. One of our other colleagues, Ingrid, was feeling annoyed at being shuffled off a Chiltern Railways train onto a Virgin one because the Chiltern train was being diverted to do something else. All that vanished, however, when further up the line the Virgin driver said over the tannoy, 'You'll be pleased to hear, ladies and gentlemen, that we've just passed the train you were meant to be on. Ha ha ha!' Everyone laughed, and all was forgiven. Once again, humour tends to thrive in a more liberal culture when staff are allowed, even encouraged, to express themselves and use their own initiative.

pause for thought...

Too strict a regime can actually create 'anti-magic', which infuriates customers rather than delighting them. Phil, one of our directors, ran up against the rather odd system of buying train tickets in Belgium. You can get a ticket on the train, as long as you signal this to the guard when you're getting on. Fail to signal, and you can get a pretty hefty fine. But how are you supposed to know this? The rules have been relaxed around the airports and major cities, where they're used to confused tourists, but out in the countryside it's a different story. A guard became quite unpleasant with Phil and relieved him of more than a few euros because he hadn't nodded in the right way at the right person when getting on the train. It wasn't as if he was trying to dodge the fare! Wouldn't it have been better if the man had simply told Phil about the rule, so he would know for next time, rather than enforcing it so rigorously?

We think that this sort of discretion ought in fact to be part of your basics. Think about your own organisation. How sure are you that your culture isn't actually encouraging people to be jobsworths?

Basics are for everyone – magic is for individuals

Magic obviously varies a lot depending on your business. A particularly special treat for members of The Wine Society might not suit the Real Ale brigade, and vice versa. So a very important thing to remember regarding magic is that you *must* know your customers – who they are, what they need, what they like. If you don't, how can you know what will delight them? Don't be fooled by memories of wonderful service that you yourself have enjoyed in the past; your special touches have to be special for your customers, not for you. The following exercise brings this point clearly to life.

exercise

TRAVELLERS' JOY

Ask a typical cross-section of people to imagine that they're on a plane or train. Get them to list what they'd expect from that service (i.e. the basics). You'll find that everyone talks about the same things: it'll be on time; they'll get a seat; the cabin/carriage will be clean; the loos will work; staff will be pleasant and able to give the right information and so on.

Then ask them to list things they think would be wonderful to have (the magic). This is likely to be a totally different story. You'll get an astonishing variety of ideas...everything from charging-up points for mobiles and laptops to robotic trolley dollies, massages and bean bags for seats. Different types of people want different things – downloads for the young, blankets for the old, bottle warmers for young families etc.

This illustrates beautifully why you need to be careful with magic. It is complicated and individual, and what might delight one person could seriously irritate another. The main lesson here is that you need to know your customer well!

Repeat the exercise with your staff about your own business. It'll give you a great insight – both into what your basics should be and into how your staff perceive your organisation.

pause for thought...

Not knowing exactly who your customers are can lead you to miss opportunities for magic. Say you're a hotel manager, for example. Instead of just checking how full your rooms are, check who is in them. A stag party? A conference-worth's of business people? Their needs and likes will be very different. One hotel we stayed in in Europe was packed with middle-aged British women who'd come over for a Cliff Richard concert. They were in high party mood. How difficult would it have been to play a few Cliff numbers at breakfast, instead of the usual hotel muzak? They'd have been enchanted!

Maintaining the sparkle

One last point to make about magic: you have to keep it fresh. Otherwise it has the potential to slide gradually down the special scale until it becomes the norm and expected by your customers – a basic in fact.

There is even a scientific theory about this called the Kano Model, developed in the eighties by Professor Noriaki Kano. In essence, the model shows that things that are new and excite customers when they are first introduced gradually become expected things over time. Satnavs are a good example of this. A few years ago they were the greatest sensational products imaginable, available only to the slickest of City sorts; now almost all new cars either have them as standard or at the very least as optional extras. They've slid to a category where a customer might actually feel faintly peeved if they *don't* get one. Providing things to entertain children in restaurants is another example: it's got to the point now where families are slightly surprised if the pot of crayons doesn't appear on the table along with their drinks.

Some industries are much more vulnerable to this effect than others – particularly anything vaguely related to technology – but whatever your business, do keep Kano in mind. Is your magic touch something that all your competitors have copied, which is now becoming old hat?

pause for thought...

You don't necessarily have to reinvent the wheel to refresh your magic. For example, many places now provide birthday cards if they know it's a customer's birthday. But instead of simply having a printed greeting inside 'from the management and staff of the Holiday Inn', how about getting the staff actually to sign it and write a little personal message? This happened to Phil's wife once, and she was much more delightfully surprised by it than she was with any of the champagne/roses/chocolates etc. that he'd arranged to have put in their room!

key learning points

- Get your basics right before you even think about magic, or you'll be wasting your time.
- Magic, if it comes on top of faulty basics, can actually get customers even more irritated than they would have been otherwise. They'll wonder why you're messing about with nonsense rather than sorting out your core business.
- There are different sorts of magic - planned, on the spot, breaking the rules, humour...and probably more.
- Even spontaneous magic can be created, or at least encouraged, if you build the right environment for it to flourish in.
- Magic needs to enchant your customers, not you.

- Breaking a few rules can create the most memorable magic moments. Live dangerously!
- Magic is special because it's unexpected. Try to keep it that way.

chapter 3
in your
customer's
shoe
(singular)

I n the last chapter, we stated that you have to know your customers before you can supply them with truly great service. You need to know how they think, feel, react, behave, live and more in order to give them exactly what they want. 'If you really want to understand a man, you must first walk a mile in his shoes', as the well-known Native American saying goes. Yes, this is absolutely true.

But before we go any further down this track, we need to issue a reminder of *why* providing great service is so important. It is not to do with making people happy or fulfilled or delighted with you (though these are fortunate side effects). The end objective of customer service is to **make money**. The better you treat your customers, the more they will rate you and therefore the more they will spend with you. This must never be forgotten.

dangerous challenge

'LET'S DO A LITTLE CROSS-DRESSING'

This is a simple exercise for you to do with your staff. Go to a charity shop and buy some cheap but different pairs of shoes – the wilder the better. Then ask your colleagues to take off one of their shoes and to put on one of the shoes you have bought. Give men a woman's shoe with very high heels and vice versa. Ask them to then take a walk around their place of work for 5 minutes and then come back. Ask them what it was like and how they felt!

The upshot of this is that you actually need to wear two different shoes – one belonging to your customer and one belonging to your business. If you've ever tried wearing odd shoes, you'll know that it can be pretty tricky to keep your balance. So this chapter is all about learning to maintain that balance and what it means for everyone involved.

pause for thought...

Comedian Billy Connolly had a pithy riposte to the quote about wearing a man's shoes. He said: 'And if you still don't understand him, who cares? He's a mile away and you've got his shoes!'

While we don't recommend adopting exactly this attitude, we do feel that – for the sake of your business and your bottom line – you should make some positive choices about who you serve and how you serve them.

WEARING THE FIRST SHOE

First let's examine what it really means to wear your customer's shoe. As discussed in the previous chapter, your ideal offering ought to include both basics and magic. Basics, being your core business, are for everyone, but magic is for individuals. So your job actually boils down to being able to treat every person you serve as an individual, in order to create the magic element of your service offering. This is an incredibly complex thing to do, since all individuals have different needs. Think of a call centre operative for a large plumbing company, for example. The first caller might be a worried old lady with a dripping tap; the next an impatient landlord wanting a boiler fixed in a rental flat; the next a harried man who's returned home to find sewage pouring from under a manhole cover...all within the space of a few minutes. Managing to meet all these needs in an appropriate way is very difficult – but truly wearing the customer's shoe means doing just this.

Sort and simplify

In order to help those on the front line, the most important thing organisations can do is to start segmenting their customer base into types of people who purchase their goods and services. This might sound obvious, and many companies are extremely good at it, but it still surprises us how little many businesses understand about their customers. One large hotel chain we know said of course they knew about their customer types – they were either business customers or leisure customers – full stop. But those leisure guests, were they families? Elderly couples? Hen parties? Special interest groups? Well, they didn't think so much about that or get that level of detail.

So, start with finding out who your customers are. Decide how to group them, then talk to your staff about them. Discuss how needs differ between each group, and the best ways of meeting those needs.

exercise

Ask your staff to list all of the different types of customer you have. Then ask them to write down what kind of service experience each one of them would like. Then ask them to write down what things they could do, that would cost nothing, to give this experience. You will be surprised at the number of customers and the inventiveness of your staff.

The next complication

OK, so you've examined your customer base closely and identified ten main types of customer who use your service – so far so good. But then everything goes to pieces, because customers change! Just one individual can be ten different types of customer, even within the same environment and circumstances.

Take a businessman coming into a hotel, for example. At check-in, he's wearing his suit and carrying his briefcase; he wants to know about ordering an early alarm call and a taxi for the morning; he wants brisk, efficient service. But once he's been up to his room and showered and changed, who is he then? Did he take off his business persona with his tie? Does he want you to tell him about email access facilities, or to discuss the football? He goes to the bar. But does he want to sit and scan the pages of the FT, or does he want a friendly chat about his day? His wife phones and he has a long talk to her and his children. Who is he when he finishes the call...still husband/dad, or has he snapped back to business guest? This continues throughout his stay, and you've no idea how he'll change or who he'll be until you encounter him in each situation. At breakfast, is he an alert, sharp-suited executive or just a sleepy man gradually waking up over his coffee?

The retail industry experiences the same issue. The same woman, dashing into the supermarket during her lunch hour from work, is a very different person from the one coming in on a Saturday with her family to do the weekly shop.

Obviously this phenomenon varies considerably depending on what industry you're in. If you run a craft or specialist interest shop, for instance, the majority of your customers are more likely to be in a particular mode – i.e. relaxed in pursuit of their hobby – and to remain in that mode throughout their visit to your outlet. But the message overall is that understanding customers, really understanding them, is extraordinarily complex.

Think about what it's like for customer-facing staff (if you're not one of them already). With our man-in-the-suit example above, they might need to be quick and efficient, friendly, informative, personal, impersonal, chatty, silent, sympathetic, tactful etc., all within the space of a few minutes, simply in order to meet his needs and demands – which, after all, is their job. That's a lot of different shoes to hop into in a very short time! Such agility might be OK for your 10 per cent of natural service givers who simply sense intuitively what is required. But for the other 90 per cent, it's a pretty tall order. So if you're a manager, don't be too hard on your staff!

Make a choice

The good news, however, is that there are things you can do to
help make life a bit easier for yourself and your staff.

The most significant is first to decide who among your
customers you really want to target for wonderful service. This
may sound controversial, but bear with us. The ones you want to
start with aren't necessarily either those who spend the most
money with you or the most numerous – they are the easiest.
Who these people are will vary depending on your product or
service, but every business will have one segment of customers
who are easier to provide with great service than any other.
This is either because their needs and wants are obvious and
straightforward, or because their situation is easy for staff to
empathise with. In hotels, it's a simple choice. Business people
are tricky because they switch constantly between business and
personal mode, as we saw above. Families, on the other hand,
are a cinch: if you are lovely to the children, the adults will think
you're wonderful. Elderly guests too provide a rewarding target
for increased effort; they tend not to be in a hurry and almost
always appreciate a friendly chat. In a supermarket, the choices
might be similar. A harried mother trying to juggle several
small children and a huge trolley-full is likely to be grateful for
unsolicited assistance with packing bags and lugging stuff out
to the car. A lost-looking bloke wandering the aisles aimlessly

may well appreciate someone offering to help find all the things on his list.

> Think about your own customers and, together with your staff, decide which ones are easiest to provide with great service. Then focus your main efforts on them.
>
> Making a positive choice in this way is a key step if you want to move your customer service up a gear or two.

Why choose?

While you may feel slightly uneasy about lumping customers into categories in this way, there is a very sound reason for providing *visibly* wonderful service – even if it is focused mainly on particular kinds of people: **giving great service is infectious.** This works in three ways:

1. Customers who *see other* customers receiving great service feel great themselves. Remember the Tesco worker in Chapter 2 who let the little blind girl sit on her lap to help 'beep' things through the till? Almost every other customer who witnessed that smiled and commented...it spread a positively rosy glow among all bystanders. So even if you're actually concentrating only on one section of your customer base, *most* of your customers will feel as if they themselves are benefitting, simply from observation.

2. In addition, customers are better primed to receive service. We've pointed out before that some customers seem to *attract* good service. This is usually because they're open and friendly themselves and more than ready to be pleased with you, if you give them the smallest reason to be so.

Customers who have witnessed you being wonderful to others are much more likely to be in this positive frame of mind, with the result that even a little effort from you will make them happy.

3. Staff who see colleagues being helpful and friendly also receive the reflected warm glow noted above, and are in turn more inclined to deliver great service too.

Simply 'seeding' excellent service throughout your organisation in this way can therefore lead to a pretty bumper harvest in terms of goodwill and increased effort!

Spot the signs

Another very useful way of deciding where to direct your service efforts is learning to spot what we call the 'signals of service'. Customers will actually tell you how they want to be served, if you know what you're looking for.

There are all kinds of interesting things we can tell you about body language and so on (and we'll go into these later in the book), but most signals are actually pretty simple. A customer whose glass is empty but who is still sitting at the table would probably like another drink; a person struggling with multiple shopping bags would most likely be glad of help getting them to the car. These are the circumstantial signs – what customers are doing, in other words. Other signs relate to state – how people *are*. Are they talking/smiling/shouting/looking lost? And the same applies here: someone examining a sofa with intense interest may well want to buy it; a cross-faced bloke may need either speedy assistance or general soothing.

It's possible to get pretty complicated on the subject of signal spotting, but the general rule is as before: look for the signals you understand and start by serving those people who are sending them.

Beware of stereotyping

Having said all these things about watching customers to see what service you can offer them, we also need to issue a warning: it is very easy to jump to conclusions about people – who they are, what they might be like, what they might need – and to be completely wrong in your judgement. The following exercise shows this perfectly.

exercise

WHO'S JIMMY?

Study the photographs below, then read the descriptions of 'Jimmy'. Which of the photos do they describe?

- People sometimes think Jimmy is unfriendly and they are intimidated by his stern expression, but he's really a big softie at heart. It's just a bit of an act for work.
- He's got a secret love of Barry Manilow's music, but dreads his colleagues finding out.
- He's never happier than when he's taking the dogs for a walk in the countryside.
- He's always fussing about getting his hair 'just so' to maintain his image.

Then do the same with 'Catherine':

- Catherine is always organising girls' nights out with her friends and she loves a gin and tonic.
- She can never remember where she put her keys so she's late for everything.
- She can't stand it when her other half retunes her radio to Classic FM.
- Her favourite items of clothing are her fluffy pink slippers.

You'll probably find that you make instant assumptions about which of the photos are being described in each case. But actually, all the descriptions could apply to either – it will simply be your own preconceptions that are making you leap to conclusions. Repeat the same exercise with your staff. It is a good way of making everyone aware of how they make automatic judgements about people. The lesson is about trying to suspend those judgements; to balance your human reactions with a more measured decision about how you will offer service. Don't assume, explore in other words. Continuing with the theme of this chapter, it's about learning to put on your customer's shoe...but slowly!

WEARING THE SECOND SHOE

When we talk about wearing your business shoe, we mean you need to keep two important things in mind. Firstly, the kind of service you offer should be dictated by the needs of your business. If you are a beautician, for example, the way you serve your customers will be absolutely crucial to the very existence of your business – so a fabulous customer experience should be your number one priority (apart from your core offering of making people look good, obviously). If you run a petrol station, the service requirements are not quite so critical, as people will purchase petrol regardless. The second element is to keep a constant eye on the effect that the service you offer has on your business. For instance, do you need more staff (or less sometimes) in order to maintain your chosen service levels? Does it lead to particular training requirements? Are you neglecting the basics of your business in pursuit of the magic? And so on.

We think there are a few important points to make about service from a business point of view that will help you to get these two elements right.

An important distinction

Companies often confuse *service* with *services*. The two, however, are very different and not understanding this properly can lead to great amounts of misdirected effort and money. Service, singular, is what this book is all about – delivering a great customer experience that will lead to loyalty, increased spend and all other good things.

Services, plural, means all the things you are offering – your products, your range, the number of things you will do for payment – regardless of whether you're a drycleaner, a pharmacy or whatever.

Too many businesses spend too much money increasing the latter in the mistaken belief that this will improve the former. But simply introducing more of this or new ones of that or increased levels of the other won't affect the service you provide. True, you may gain new customers because of your new services, and your existing customers may appreciate them. But the bottom line is that the interaction between your business and your customers will remain unaffected. So think carefully before investing heavily in new services. Could the same gain be achieved by focusing your attention more carefully on service without the 's'?

The perfect match

We touched on this point briefly in Chapter 1, but it's very important and will bear frequent repetition.

It is possible to give five-star service in a two-star hotel. Just because a product is basic, that doesn't mean the service attached to it has to be basic. In fact, an economy product or service has far greater potential to create surprise and delight – i.e. magic – for a customer than a premium one does, because it is far easier to exceed expectations. So quality of service and quality of services do not have to match. In fact you can change your customers' whole perception of your services and, by extension, your brand, by providing them with a higher level of service than they might have anticipated. The catalogue company Hawkins Bazaar is a great example of this. The items they offer are actually quite commonplace and cheap in quality but they sell them by the thousand to discerning customers, partly because they concentrate on making their catalogue really funny, lively and unusually human in feel, and partly because their service is fabulous. Orders arrive almost before the customer is off the phone, postage isn't charged for, errors are corrected instantly and callers always get a real person when they ring rather than horrible lists of menus from an electronic voice.

Together, the two points above lead to an interesting question for all business groups and multi-brand companies:

> Should there be a core set of service values at the heart of everything offered, despite the fact that services vary considerably?

In other words, should customers expect to receive the same service experience buying from Skoda as they do from Porsche (both now being part of the VAG group), for example? And what about Virgin: should their service to customers be exactly the same, regardless of whether the customer is buying a flight to the US or the latest Scratch Perverts CD?

Service is service

It is easy to feel rather squeamish about providing wonderful service to people in order to get them to spend more money. Alternatively, it can also be tempting to become truly manipulative in the efforts you make to get customers to part with their cash. As always, there is a balance to be struck.

We see it like this. As we said at the beginning of the chapter, the essential end purpose of customer service is to create loyalty and to maintain or increase revenue. There is simply no arguing with this, as without decent revenue your business will cease to exist. There is therefore no need to be afraid of using all reasonable means at your disposal to optimise sales, and 'up-selling' is a great way to go. *Always* make the offer to bring another bottle of wine to the restaurant table, to find a tie to go with that shirt, to change the oil in the car while you're doing its MOT. And yes, the National Trust and other organisations are absolutely right to channel visitors through their shops before they can reach the exit. Service designed to sell is still service. And if people didn't want to be sold to or to spend their money, they wouldn't be in your shop or on your website, would they?

So while you probably ought to stop short of getting your customers in a headlock until they give in and agree to buy, or forcibly turning out their pockets for them, you can adopt this as your new mantra:

(Supersizing is OK, yeah!)

Switch on your service senses

In addition to absorbing the previous three points into the whole way you think about service, there are a couple of things you can do that will help you and your staff to brush up your service skills. For starters, you can 'switch on your service senses' – tune into the service being given by others, in other words. This doesn't necessarily entail examining what your competitors do, it means learning actively to notice all the service you receive in all areas of your life. Almost every encounter with another person outside your home involves some form of service, and learning to analyse these encounters can teach you a great deal. Just why exactly were you so cross with the bin men last week – because of the way they spoke to you, or because they left rubbish in the road? How did you feel when the doctor's receptionist was somewhat frosty about giving you an appointment? Speaking to the school secretary always makes you feel cheerful...why?

Moving into observation mode like this can give you all sorts of ideas about what you can incorporate into, or eliminate from, your own service. It's important to encourage your staff to switch on their senses too, as it'll help them to become more aware of how they themselves interact with customers.

pause for thought...

Try holding a weekly 5-minute meeting with your staff, asking them to bring along examples of the best and worst service they have received during the week.

dangerous Challenge

'LET YOUR STAFF GO SHOPPING IN THE COMPANY'S TIME'

We have found one of the best ways to switch on you and your staff's service senses is to do a 'service safari'. This is an intensive ½ or 1 day experience where you put staff into small groups and set them a series of service challenges for them to complete in local retailers. You don't need to pre-arrange anything with the shops beforehand. The most important thing is to set up the purpose with your staff before they go and bring them back together at the end of the session to discuss what they found and what this means for the service they give.

Be your own customer

When we worked with Accor hotels, we discovered that very few of their staff had ever stayed as ordinary guests in the brand of hotel they worked for, so they had no idea what it was like to be on the receiving end of the experience they gave to customers.

This is one of the easiest things you can do: provide some formal means for yourself and your staff to be customers of your own business. You will then have a much better idea of what expectations customers will have of you, and of how to meet those expectations.

pause for thought...

Many big organisations have 'friends and family' schemes, whereby their staff can use the business's services but under special conditions. They may get preferential mortgage rates, if the company is a bank, or discounted prices if it's a retailer. But is this really such a good idea? They never find out what it's actually like to be a real customer of that business – which might actually be more useful to them in the long run!

key learning points

- In order to provide magic service, you must truly understand your customer. But at the same time, the needs of your business must never be forgotten. You therefore need to wear two different shoes – one belonging to your customer and one to your business.
- Truly understanding customers is tricky, as their needs change constantly.
- It helps to simplify things. Choose which customers you understand best and start by providing them with your magic service.
- 'Seeding' good service leads to a bumper harvest in terms of customer satisfaction and goodwill.
- Learn to spot the 'signals of service' given off by people.
- Service, singular, and services, plural, are very different things. More of the latter does not improve the former.
- It's possible to give premium service in an economy business.
- Service designed to sell is still service.
- Observing the service you yourself receive in your daily life, plus becoming your own customer, are two useful ways to raise your awareness of the service you provide.

chapter 4
managing for great service

HOW DIFFERENT IS SERVICE LEADERSHIP?

Right, so now we need to talk about leadership for customer service.

If you're in any kind of management position, whether it's a team leader within a department or a chief executive of a mega organisation, how do you lead and enable your staff to deliver the kind of service you want them to deliver?

Is leadership for service any different from other kinds of leadership? And are there any particular skills which will help you to achieve the results you're after?

For starters, we think that service leadership *is* a bit different – the main point being that your 'end product', i.e. service, is somewhat intangible. It is about great interactions between people.

Traditional leadership is based on tough performance management: setting targets, giving incentives, monitoring results, holding people to account – maybe with a spice of fear added to the mix. However, this may create a culture of relationships that may not work effectively when trying to revolutionise the service in your organisation. But before we start to get too warm and fluffy about the management styles needed for great service, as we've said before, the reason we need to give great service is due to the bottom line results that must be delivered (usually through strong performance management).

So, service leadership must be combined with performance management, otherwise we will all be happy at work, creating great working relationships with staff and customers, but not gaining any sales!

Being a leader for service, therefore, is a complex thing to do. And because 'service' is intangible and all to do with people and relationships, it requires a degree of passion and commitment from those who provide it. Any member of staff, from cleaner to CEO, who doesn't much care about what they're doing will find it impossible to give great service.

We've got an interesting example of this among our clients. The head of one of the big hotel chains we work with used to be the finance director of another hotel chain. He's a great guy, but he'll tell you himself that his heart is really in numbers – he lights up when the conversation revolves around results and figures and turnover, but he struggles to maintain his enthusiasm when the discussion turns to service. And as a result, the hotels are run fantastically efficiently; costs are completely under control; he knows down to the last penny where his ROI stands, what is spent on each employee/customer/room. However, the service ethos within his hotel chain has suffered. It is not his passion, therefore it is not his people's passion. And thus it's not as good as it could be.

THE SERVICE CHAIN

This leads us on to another important aspect of service, which has consequences for how it should be led.

We talked in Chapter 2 about how 80 per cent of the way customers perceive a company is formed in the last three feet – i.e. at the moment of transaction, the moment when the staff member serves the customer. And it's true, this *is* a very important moment. So organisations pour money and time into training the staff who handle it, investing in tools to improve it, getting customer feedback on what happened and what the staff member's attitude was like, etc. etc. Yes, – it's important to do all these things (and the next chapter is our take on how to train your staff brilliantly) – **but** – too many organisations *only* focus on this interaction when trying to improve service. They are missing the key (and bleeding obvious, when you say it) point: that this final interaction between staff and customer is only the last link in a long service chain.

Behind the employee who smiles nicely at customers, says 'hello, how can I help?', serves them professionally and knowledgeably and gives them the right change, is a whole line of other people who enable them to create that moment of interaction. There's their line manager, their manager's manager, the regional manager, the national manager, the director of customer service, the chief executive...and that's without mentioning the logistics people, the delivery people, the HR people, the IT people, the suppliers and buyers and hirers and firers and chief cooks and bottle washers.

And the whole chain is only as strong as its weakest link. Take an employee on the till. Say, for example, that their manager had cancelled their last two one-to-one meetings (due to being too busy); the employee's requests for a replacement for a worn-out uniform have gone ignored, and last month Accounts had missed all of their overtime so their wages were low. How likely is it that this employee will go out of their way to provide wonderful service to the next demanding customer who comes along? Not very, we'd suggest. On the other hand, if their manager had said something great about their performance the previous day; HR had acknowledged their request for a new uniform and explained that new supplies were on order but hadn't arrived yet, and Accounts had phoned before this employee had received their wage slip, apologised about the missing overtime and told them that they were raising a cheque for them in the next two days, their customers would be much more likely to experience friendly, proactive service from them.

The whole thing is a chain reaction, in other words, with role modelling going on all the way through. As one link in the chain acts efficiently, so does the next, and the next...right through to the customer at the end.

The following exercise is a great way of illustrating this service chain and how it behaves. Try it with your staff.

exercise

CHAIN GANG

You'll need a long, thin stick...something like a garden cane would be perfect.

Get your team to form a line, side by side, all holding the stick. Give each person a name/role – customer, staff member, manager, director, chief executive etc. (whatever's most appropriate to your business). Then get whoever is the customer to start moving the stick – up, down, side to side, wherever they like. The others must relax their hands and go with the flow, following whatever the customer does. You should find that the whole team moves easily in synch, almost like a sort of dance.

Next, though, get one or more of the others – the store manager and the chief executive, say – to start resisting or trying to move the stick in a different direction. You'll see tugging and tension and rivalry. Do it vigorously enough and you'll end up with everyone on the floor and a broken stick – end of service chain!

Customer ⟺ Staff ⟺ Manager ⟺ Executive

the service chain

Polishing the chain

Some companies *do* actually recognise the importance of this service chain, and as a consequence tend to be among the very best service providers in the country. As usual, for example, John Lewis scores highly in this regard. Yes, yes, we know – that their staff are all partners in the business, which means they truly take ownership of their jobs, which in turn helps to create great service. It's true that this partnership model has a lot to do with staff performance. But at the same time, team leaders work with and coach those on the shop floor. Their managers in turn do the same on a whole-store basis. Every structure in place within the whole organisation is designed to care for the partners. Result: the staff in turn really care about their customers and the company is regularly voted top for customer service in retail.

O2 has taken this attention to the chain even further. In their call centres, surprisingly, they provide very little training to staff on customer service. Instead, the focus is on creating the best possible working environment – with coaching, support mechanisms, fun events and benefits that are second to none. This has resulted in conditions and an environment that people love to work in: staff turnover in call centres is less than 1 per cent. The company measures and monitors *everything* – each person's time is split into 15-minute blocks that have to be accounted for, supervisors constantly walk the floors and so on – but staff still love it. 'They really care about us' is the general comment. 'If we are taking too long to do something, they don't come and give us a hard time – they show us new ways to do things more quickly.' And because the people are so positive and engaged, the relationship with customers takes care of itself. Interestingly enough, O$_2$ provides *massive* training for managers. They are monitored on the coaching they do, the feedback they give, how positive their attitudes are...all the investment is in this area.

The same principle applies at the opposite end of the service spectrum. Staff who work for Ryanair (yes, them again) are *not* interested in giving service. Don't expect them to be. Their whole culture is about cost, cost, cost and to charge for everything (including going to the toilet on the plane). So this ethos is relected all the way down the service chain, mirroring the company's vision and focus. The service you'll receive is therefore simple, single-minded and clear: this is what we offer, take it or leave it – and we don't particularly care if you don't like it.

As we said at the start of this chapter, for most of us who aren't John Lewis and aren't Ryanair, service leadership balanced with performance management are sometimes uneasy bedfellows.

SKILLS AND SUPPORT STRUCTURES

All of this goes to show just how important you are, as a link in the chain. Everyone can influence the strength of their part of the chain. Where you lead, the rest of the chain will follow. So the place to start, when thinking about service leadership, is with yourself.

To be a truly great service leader, you need to know where service sits in your value set. If some other aspect of management – sales and revenue, say – completely dominates your thinking, you need to think very hard about whether it should be you who is in charge of service within your team.

dangerous Challenge

GIVE YOURSELF THE SERVICE BOOT

Everyone in business says they care about service. But do you? Be truthful! If it's not what floats your boat, don't lead a service team. Get someone else to do it. Or at the very least, recognise this in yourself and delegate as much responsibility for service as you can to a colleague who does care, and who you can listen to and respect.

Once you've established whether or not it should be you in charge of service, you need to think about how you, your team, your department and your organisation support service. There are two sides to this...we like to think of them as the 'software' and 'hardware' of service leadership.

- 'Software' is the intangibles – the skills, attitudes and behaviours that lead to wonderful service.
- 'Hardware' is the mechanical side of service leadership – the processes and structures that support it and make it flow smoothly.

Service leadership software
There are three types of service leadership software: visioning, role modelling and coaching.

Get to people's passion through visioning
First and foremost among the service software you require is visioning. You might think this means 'creating a vision', but it is more than this. Visioning is a continual process. If you are not constantly renewing the vision and maintaining people's enthusiasm in it, there is a danger that it will drift – even if the vision is a good one. You need to have everyone telling stories about it and keep enrolling and re-enrolling people in it. To make visioning really effective, there are two important rules:

1. Make it simple. For example, O2's vision is to 'turn customers into fans'. This is a *huge* aspiration, as there has to be true emotional engagement for someone to transform from a customer into a fan, but it's an attractive idea and everyone gets it straight away.

2. Make it appeal to all parts of your staff's humanity. The really good service leader will find ways to link a vision to all of the following aspects of character:

a. Reason (heads) – e.g. link the provision of great service to pay and promotions, rewards and recognition.

b. Emotion (hearts) – e.g. encourage a feeling of pride and achievement about providing great service.

c. Physical (bodies) – e.g. leap up off your seat and demonstrate physically what the vision is...mime it, role play it, act it out – and then get staff to show *you* in return what it means to them.

d. Spiritual (souls) – e.g. make the provision of great service appeal to people's inner values, such as making the world a better place/adding to the sum total of happiness etc.

As we've said already, unless people are truly involved in the idea of giving great service, it is difficult for them to do it well. Visioning, therefore, is key in capturing their imagination and getting their buy-in from the outset.

Role modelling
The next vital piece of service leadership software you need in your kit is role modelling. We talked about how one link in the chain tends to behave in the same way as the previous link. So – as the leader – this starts with you. And there are two areas in which to do it:

1. With customers in front of staff. *Always* deliver to customers what you want your staff to deliver. Don't worry about knowing the technical detail. Behind the bar, for instance, you may not be able to tell the difference between Bell's and Laphroaig (it's all whisky, isn't it?), but you can see that the customer wants a drink. So you

must get in there and sort it out...even if that just means going to find the person who *does* know what's required. Attitude is all in this case – don't ignore the customer, just go and do! In our job, we are lucky enough to visit lots of different organisations and frequently get shown round stores, hotels, restaurants etc. by members of the senior executive team. We've lost count of the number of times we've been standing there in a store surrounded by customers looking for assistance, listening to our hosts who – while completely ignoring what's going on about us – complain away about how none of their staff are proactive in approaching customers!

2. In the way you treat your staff. 'Do as you would be done by' may be the sort of thing your Gran used to say when you were little, but it's really important when talking about service. You need to deal with every person as you would wish them to deal with you, and in the same way as you would wish them to deal with a colleague or customer. Think about how you behave to people wanting your attention when you're busy. How long do you make someone wait before you look up? Do you stop what you're doing and give your colleague your full concentration?

Coaching

Now we come to *the* most vital part of leading for great service: coaching. It is the grandfather of them all, the skill you require more than any other. Use it properly and you can transform even a truculent bunch of work-experience school leavers into service providers *par excellence*.

OK, so what is coaching?

It's not counselling, but neither is it a casual chat. It's appropriate feedback and encouragement to people that guides and enthuses them in the way that they do their jobs, that's what. And as you can see from the graph below, it's much more effective than training on its own.

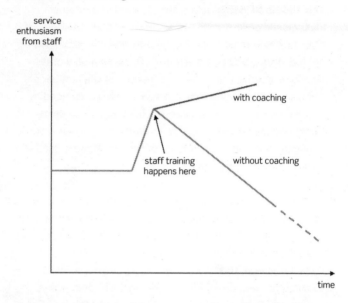

This is because people tend to feel all immediately excited and energised by a training session, only to slip and slide gradually down the 'oh why should I bother' hill again afterwards because it's not followed up. With coaching, however, they receive regular little boosts which maintain them at a less dramatic but higher overall level.

Before we go any further with this, we need to pause to explode a common myth. Many managers we talk to immediately say something like, 'I don't think I'd be very good at coaching – I'm not the right sort of person'. There's a general perception that coaches are calm, all-wise, all-knowing, patient, teacher sorts of people – that there is an ideal 'coach personality'. But this is complete nonsense. Do the exercise below and you'll believe us!

exercise

THE IDEAL COACH?

Give yourself five minutes to write down the names of all the coaches you can think of. This can be any kind of coach, but footballing ones are the most famous so we'll use them by way of example.

Say on your list you've got:

- Sven-Göran Eriksson
- Jürgen Klinsmann
- Alex Ferguson
- Kevin Keegan.

You then write down the main characteristics of each:

- a cool cucumber;
- a shouter and frother;
- a roarer;
- a terrier.

Look at your second list. Do you think they're all the same type of person? No! But are they all good coaches? Well you can argue with your friends about whether or not you agree with them, but they *must* all be top class to be coaching for their countries or some of the best teams in the world!

All of which goes to prove that *any* type of person can be a good coach. You don't have to have particular characteristics, you can do it from your own personality. It's more a question of using the right techniques...for which read on!

There's probably been more wordage written on coaching than on any other business skill, so we're not going to go into enormous detail here about all the different forms it can take. What we *will* do, though, is to give you our coaching model. The great thing about this is that it is equally suited to formal 20-minute coaching sessions as it is to 1-second 'coaching shoot-outs', depending on how much time you've got available. So here it is.

Kite Coaching Process

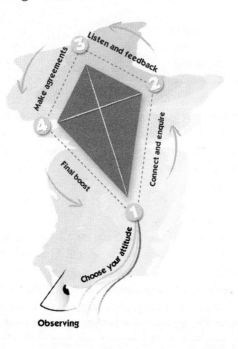

Observing

Observe – You need to watch staff in action, seeing exactly what's going on with your own eyes. It's really important not to rely on hearsay about how someone performs, although you can support your observations with feedback from customers or colleagues.

Choose your attitude – It's important to make sure you're in the right frame of mind before you hold a coaching session. If you're too tired or stressed or anything else, your own emotions/ state of mind will get in the way and the coaching won't be effective. It would be much better to reschedule the session. This is particularly the case if the person you're coaching has done something to annoy you. By all means yell, 'Look, you've got customers waiting!' to someone having a sneaky fag outside when they're meant to be serving, but wait until the end of the shift to express your disappointment with their behaviour in a balanced kind of way!

Connect and enquire – There is one essential opening line: 'So how do you think that went then?' Not only is this an unthreatening start, enabling the person being coached to feel like a partner in the process, you'll also get a much better insight into his or her approach and what their natural service level is. *You* might have thought Maureen from HR was being a grump; *she* might have thought she was being brisk and efficient. This in turn will tell you what level of coaching the person will require from you.

Listen and feedback – (this is where most people start). All feedback must be based on data – real facts or observations – not on your opinions. What you say is then rooted in truth and means the person is both less inclined to argue with you and more inclined to think about why you said it. If, on finding that your trainee has locked the door on leaving, as instructed, but left all the windows wide open, which do you think is the better thing to say: 'Rachel, I think you're a chump!', or 'Rachel, I notice that you left the windows open...was there a particular reason for that?'

Make agreements – Any subsequent actions again need to be referred back to the person being coached. Instead of bawling

'You need to clean up your act, young man!', it is much better to ask 'What are you going to do about it?' or 'How do you think you will handle this next time?'. The solution needs to come from them, and then you both agree to it and, if appropriate, set a time frame.

Final boost – Finish with something really encouraging. 'You can do this. I've seen you being fantastic with lots of children, and I know you'll manage not to lose your temper next time the Simpson twins climb up on your counter...'

Check back – It's also important to follow up on the agreed actions, whether or not you've put a 'when by' on it. People are much more likely to up their game if they know their efforts will be noticed.

And that's it. As we said, this model adapts well to different levels of intensity, depending on particular coaching needs. We tend to use three levels:

- Level 1: A planned session of between 15 and 20 minutes.
- Level 2: 30-second on the job coaching, to be done immediately whenever you notice something, whether good or bad. It follows the same cycle as above: 'I saw...', 'What did you think?', feedback, 'What will you do next time?', 'Fantastic – if anyone can do it, you can...'.
- Level 3: 1-second positive coaching. This can be thought of as 'coaching on the touchline' and it's *all* encouraging... 'I saw that, well done!' It's quite a difficult thing to do as it can make you feel self-conscious and/or somewhat parental, but it really does work. It's an instant energiser for the person receiving it, so do it as much as you can!

exercise

THE 1-SECOND COACHING SHOOT-OUT

Learning to give 1-second positive coaching is an excellent skill for a whole team to have. People learn to look out for and appreciate the good in each other and it's brilliant for building team spirit.

We think this exercise works best if you do it, say, on a team awayday, when you can start by splitting everyone into two teams and playing some fun, lightly competitive games. We often play baseball, for instance. The important thing is to get everyone to notice how they behave: with no shame or embarrassment, almost everybody will shout and yell encouragement to each other, jump up and down cheering, whoop and clap and punch the air – all quite naturally.

What you then want to do is to recreate that atmosphere during the exercise!

Keeping everyone in their teams, give them all one minute to write down every single way they can think of to encourage each other in a work environment – verbally, by hand signals, body language, everything – and then ask each team to amalgamate all the ideas into one list. The two teams then line up facing each other and literally do a 'shoot-out', shouting all the compliments from their lists at each other one by one... 'thumbs up!', 'high five!', 'pat on the back', 'well done!', 'go girl!' – and so on, until one team runs out.

We give everyone cowboy hats while they're doing this, and it is usually completely hilarious...and **fantastic** at creating a positive atmosphere. Not surprisingly after this, people also seem to be much less inhibited about handing out the praise during their normal working day!

And a final word on coaching.... For now at least

(Coaching is for everyone!
(Not just your poor performers))

A number of organisations we have worked with have started with a belief that coaching was only for those problem staff... No, no, no! Every member of staff should be coached: remember that coaching is to reinforce and praise as well as support and correct.

(And if everyone is being coached then those who are difficult are not being singled out.)

Service leadership hardware

When we talk about structures here, let us be clear. We do not mean logistics or nuts and bolts. We assume that you have those in place already. After all, a cash till that is not kept sufficiently stocked with change is a fat lot of use to anyone really. And a delivery company that does not maintain its vans properly cannot expect peak performance from its drivers. If you haven't got the mechanics of your business sorted, you probably won't stay in business very long.

Help or hindrance?

What we're talking about is the spirit of your structures. Do the processes in your organisation help people to provide great service or hinder them from doing so? Say, for example, you're the manager of a hotel. Why did you choose to become the manager of a hotel? It was probably because you like dealing with people. But what do you spend most of your day doing? Paperwork and admin, most likely, which have nothing to do with serving people. The police are always complaining that they spend so long doing paperwork that they don't have much time for catching criminals!

It is really important, therefore, to evaluate how the processes you have in place support service. Do they match what you say you value most?

Build your service leadership into your process

The other essential thing about structures is that they need to be used to ensure that you keep the focus on service. You need to consistently build service into your routine operations. Take team meetings, for instance. Most companies have them regularly. But is service on the team meeting agenda? Usually not! We have some Belgian clients who were having trouble sustaining their SSWAS (service starts with a smile) ethos. So we helped them to build service into all their regular structures. It's on the agenda for every single meeting; there's a whole calendar of SSWAS events with staff (they all go bowling in the most SSWAS way possible, for instance, and they have SSWAS cakes on Fridays!). Little markers and events like this need to be regular to give people energy and maintain their enthusiasm.

In the same way, make sure you build coaching time into your plans. One of the O2 measures for managers is the number of coaching sessions they give to staff, and the feedback received from their coachees. It's not a case of doing it when you have time or when you feel like it – it needs to be one of the foundation stones of your calendar.

The Ritz Carlton hotels are renowned for their superb service. And once you look at the routine there, you can see why. The chain has a service 'Credo', consisting of 20 different service points. At the beginning of every day, there is a stand-up meeting for all staff in all hotels, when they choose one of these points to focus on. What are they going to do about this point today? How are they going to embody it in the service they offer their customers? What will make it obvious they're doing it? And so on.

The point is that you simply cannot stress service too much. Label it, connect it up with all your activities, name people's roles and responsibilities in terms of service. It is all about making *everyone* responsible, from accounts to maintenance. And then, of course, you need to measure it and reward it...but these are so important we've devoted a whole chapter to them. Read on!

key learning points

- Leadership for great service is complex. Because service is about delivering an experience through your people, it requires an emotional 'buy-in' from the leader that isn't necessarily required in other circumstances.
- Service does *not* consist solely of the moment of transaction with the customer. It is a whole chain of service moments that runs throughout a whole organisation.
- The service chain is only as strong as its weakest link. All it takes is for one person in that chain to pull in a different direction and the whole thing falls apart.
- It is therefore more important to take care of the whole chain than just to pour investment into training the people who handle the final transaction with the customer.
- As head of the chain, all links will follow your lead. So do you really truly care about service, or should you delegate responsibility for it to someone who does?
- Your skills and your company's structures should all be geared to supporting service.
- The three most important skills are visioning, role modelling and coaching.
- Structures should be modified to help service, not hinder it, and to maintain everyone's focus on it all the time.

chapter 5
creating service heroes

Over the last few years, there's been a change in thinking about service givers. Employers and recruiters have become more likely to regard attitude as being more important than skills...'If this person has the right attitude, we can easily train them in the skills they need to provide brilliant service'...kind of thing. And to some extent they're right. As we've already said, there *are* people who are naturally good at interacting with others and giving great service. But this leaves companies with a big problem. Natural service givers are rare (only about 10 per cent of the workforce) so there aren't enough to go round. And if you've already got staff (and if you're reading this book, you probably have), what are you meant to do? Sack them all and start again with the 'right' sort? Hardly!

We think – in fact we know – that there are many many things you can do to help the 90 per cent of the workforce who are *not* natural service givers to become real service heroes. So that's what this chapter is about. We're going to explode a couple of major myths about service giving and give you practical, everyday tools that will help your staff to provide wonderful service *without* major upheaval, either to them as individuals or to your organisation as a whole.

THE MYTHS
Myth number one: We need more staff

When we ask managers what is the main barrier to providing fabulous service, almost all of them – regardless of seniority or industry sector – tell us that they don't have enough people. 'We're rushed off our feet,' they say, 'we simply don't have time for frills'.

We haven't quite got to the stage where we say 'rubbish!' as our initial response, but we're not far off. The fact is, there is such a thing as *too many* staff as illustrated in the following example.

Phil once arrived at a hotel reception to check in as a guest. It was nice and quiet in the lobby and there was no one else waiting. There were two receptionists, one at either end of the long desk, both tapping away busily at their computers. Normally what you'd do is to choose one of them to approach, and he or she would probably look up immediately.

On this occasion, though, Phil decided to stand right at the centre of the desk, just for the hell of it. What do you think happened?

What happened was that neither receptionist looked up. Phil stood there for quite some minutes, until things started to get embarrassing, then 'ahem-ed' at one of them – who of course was immediately all smiles and helpfulness.

The point is, if there'd been only one receptionist at the desk, Phil wouldn't have stood there smiling to himself and tapping his foot for so long. The receptionist would have recognised straight away that it was *their* responsibility to attend to Phil. It's human nature to think 'oh, someone else will do it', if there's someone else about.

In addition, whenever we ask staff themselves when they give their best service, they always say 'when we're busy'. Being busy creates an energy, a momentum, that makes service flow better and more efficiently. People get into the 'zone'. When things are quiet, one of two things happens: either boredom sets in and energy and efficiency drop, or staff occupy themselves doing other things like stock-taking, shelf-stacking or talking to each other. Either way, service suffers as customers are no longer the priority.

Before you start protesting, we know that there *is* a relationship between levels of service and levels of busyness. Obviously there is – and obviously there is such a thing as being too busy. We'll talk about ways of dealing with this in a minute. First though, here's another myth.

Myth number two: Attitude is more important than skills

Yes, we do actually think this is another myth. We used to believe it but we changed our minds, thanks to an interesting experiment we did that blew up in our faces.

When we were working with Accor, we agreed to try a new way for recruiting new staff for a new hotel: we'd run a recruitment day looking specifically for people with the right attitude, regardless of whether they'd worked in the hotel industry or not. Accor had unusual restaurants, in that they were all about the whole dining experience: they served food on wooden plates; they took big blackboards to the tables for diners to order from; with house wine, they put out whole bottles then charged customers for however much they'd drunk...and so on. So it seemed like a great plan to find staff who could really add to the fun and atmosphere of the experience.

We had a fantastic recruitment day in a theatre, getting candidates up on stage doing a turn, interviewing them about the interesting things they'd done in their lives etc., and ended up with a terrific bunch of people from all kinds of backgrounds. It was all very exciting.

But six months later, every single one of those people had left. Why? One word: process. They could do the attitude, but they'd been floored by the practicalities. What size glass do you need for white wine? Should you pour it out? Who should you pour it for first? Should you fill the glass? Where do you put napkins? How do you work the till? Can this lady have the salad without dressing?

We had completely underestimated the skills required, and without any experience our poor recruits had been stressed to the point that their attitude didn't count any more. They simply didn't have the tools to do the job.

Staff turnover in some businesses can be huge. For example, we know of hotels where it's around 200 per cent! And it's probably even higher in places like fast food kitchens and catalogue company warehouses. There simply isn't time to train all new starters from scratch, however good their attitude. You need to get them started really quickly, in which case they have to have the right skills.

SOME PRACTICALITIES

Now the myths are out of the way, it's time to get on to some practicalities. Let's start by re-stating your position:

'I've got too few staff; I've got too little time; our service is OK but making it brilliant is just one frill that I can do without.' (See, we *do* understand your concerns.)

But actually you don't need more staff, and you don't need more time to make your service brilliant. You can achieve this without increasing either. The secret is to incorporate the elements that make for brilliant service into all the activities that you do already.

Here's an example. Do you remember in Chapter 2 when we told you how delighted Simon was to be told about the history of the lovely hotel he was staying in? This illustrates our point perfectly. It was obviously part of the hotel's *normal* process to take guests up to their rooms. So it took no extra time at all to tell Simon fascinating details on the way...with the result that he was completely charmed and remembers it as one of the best places he's ever stayed.

So, the first, most significant thing you can do to up the ante on your service is to:

Build excellent service into your processes

The important thing about process is that it provides the framework in which service can take place. By its very nature, it should deliver a reasonable level of service. Your customer should leave you with whatever it was he or she wanted to obtain from you and feeling reasonably good about it. Mrs Brown has got her loaf of bread, in a bag, plus the right change, and it all happened pretty quickly. That's the minimum.

Beyond this, there are various elements of the process you can look at in order to make that service more special.

Order

In John Lewis, it is the order in which service happens that matters. When Mr White enters an area of the store, he is acknowledged by a member of staff – just a smile and a 'hello'. It is only if he stays in that area for more than a few moments that he is asked if he needs any help. John Lewis has understood that customers can feel hassled if they are approached with offers of help too soon. So in this instance, it's the order in which things are done that is the foundation of excellent service.

Simplicity

Asda has a very simple 'three-foot rule'. As staff walk down the aisles, they say hello to everyone who comes within three feet of them. That's it. Again, this is a process which specifically enables service to be given. If customers want help, the way is clear for them to ask for it.

Structure

For Accor staff, the process is: 'Stand up, Smile, Say hello'. Even for people who don't find service natural, this is very easy to remember and to do – and once again it immediately paves the way for service to follow. While you do want to guard against robotic service (there's been a huge kickback against the whole 'have-a-nice-day' thing), putting a structure in place is really important, as it allows service to flow naturally on from it.

Additions

We talked about the 'showing Simon round the hotel' example above. Here's another one. All supermarkets (that we know of) get their staff to take customers who are looking for specific items to the right aisle. Often, the member of staff zooms ahead, with the customer puffing along behind trying not to run over people with their trolley. How much extra time would it take to walk alongside the customer and have a little chat? 'It's pasta you're looking for...what kind of pasta? Oh, are you having a party?' – and so on. This might turn out to be simply a friendly chat, but it might also result in further sales: wine, to go with the pasta; basil, to put in the sauce; a pan, to put the pasta in, etc. In any event, it is giving the customer more – attention, interest, friendly human interaction – without taking up any extra time.

Simon came across a great example the other day in Hawkins Bazaar. He was just paying for his purchases when the girl on the till said, 'Lots of people who've bought that gizmo have loved this gadget too!' (holding up another item for him to see). She was doing an Amazon on him, and he was really impressed. Not only would this be great for Hawkins' sales, but as a customer he felt that she'd really taken an interest in his likes and preferences. And again, it took no longer than an ordinary till transaction.

To sum up then, great service does not equal extra time – it just needs to start in the right way. So take a look at your processes and see where you can add in the little magic ingredients to things you already do. It can make a **huge** difference – out of all proportion – to the way customers perceive your service.

> Major lesson
> The important thing to note about all this is that it is **process** that enables great service to be given by the majority of your staff, *not* natural ability on the part of the service giver!

Show people how to behave

After process, the next most important thing to work on with your staff is behaviour. In other words, not just what they do but how they do it. We get protests when we talk to clients about this...'But isn't it obvious that you shouldn't shout across the shop/ talk on your mobile when serving/argue in front of customers?' etc.

Actually, no it isn't. We don't know why this is – changes in society, less emphasis on manners, the 'me first' generation... whatever. We're not getting into that, and it doesn't really matter here anyway. What we *do* know though is that you need to tell your staff exactly what you expect of them in terms of behaviour.

And this needs to be clear and simple. The last thing busy people need is complicated instructions to remember while they're rushing around. At Tesco, for example, they've set a very straightforward set of behaviours that they ask of their staff: 'Know your stuff; Show you care; Share a smile'. And this is absolutely all that is required, on top of the process stuff. You don't even need to fill in the blanks...you ask people to think about how *they'd* show they care.

This last point is important. While, as we've said, you *do* need to tell people how you want them to behave, you also need to allow them to be responsible for their own behaviour. At the Bromford Housing Association, who win awards for the service they give their tenants, they have a set of service expressions, the last of which is 'Add a bit of you'. This makes it explicit that staff can still be themselves – in fact they must still be themselves – and share their humanity with their customers. This takes care of the robotic service problem in one stroke.

The key issue is to release people, but within safe boundaries. This was a difficult cultural shift for Tesco, to allow staff to move away from set scripts and trust them to behave appropriately. But they soon recognised that by providing guidelines and support rather than iron chains, staff were free to fly – and the standard of customer service shot up!

TACKLING THE SERVICE PLATEAU

For most people, giving service is almost like a journey. From whatever their starting point, they travel up a process learning slope (i.e. they acquire the knowledge and skills they require for their jobs) until they reach a nice smooth plateau...their comfort level. Many people then stay here for ever more, jogging along peacefully and operating at a competent, if unexciting, level. Not too bad, if all you want to achieve is a competent level of service. But in this book we're talking about fantastic, fabulous, outstanding service – so you're going to have to find ways of encouraging those people to keep climbing the hill, onwards and upwards.

So, how do you help your staff to come off their comfortable perches and keep climbing? We have a whole pack of cards up our sleeves on this one, so here are some of the aces. The first, and most essential, is:

Training

We talked a lot in the last chapter about the service chain, and about how some companies focus too much of their effort on training front-line staff when really they should be concentrating on getting the whole chain to function properly.

That said though, you do need to equip the people providing the service directly to the customer with the right tools. Our poor 'attitude recruits' fell apart because they didn't have suitable skills, remember. However, there is training and training – and companies in the UK waste an enormous amount of money on training that isn't actually fit for purpose. So we think there are two main things you need to consider before committing your training budget.

1. Make it bespoke to your business

One of the biggest complaints we hear from staff is that the training they've received doesn't apply to them. We cannot stress strongly enough that **generic training does not work!** It needs to be about your people and your organisation. Every example, every exercise, every message needs to be rooted in the daily lives of your staff. In this way, people can translate what they learn into exactly what they need to do in their own jobs. There is no point floating a lot of theory and ideas without demonstrating how to apply them in real situations that staff recognise as being relevant to themselves. So if you're talking about customers for instance, make sure it's about your own customers – who they are, what they want, what works, what doesn't, what Stella in Accounts did that was so great, why all the old ladies love Bernard the trolley man so much...you get the picture.

2. Make it little and often

One of the reasons we're so in favour of coaching is that it can be given in small, frequent chunks that keep the recipient's energy and enthusiasm levels boosted all the time. As far as possible, the same should apply to training. Before you protest and say 'but it's an enormous undertaking, training all our branch staff in the new computer system – we can't possibly do this little and often!', don't worry, we know. There are occasions when only a massive, blanket-coverage training programme will fit the bill. But most kinds of training can actually be done in a different way – what we call 'action training'.

This is how it works. You train each of your managers in whatever it is you want everyone to know – either all together or separately, depending on practicalities. Then you get each of those managers to hold training sessions for small groups of staff, drawn from different areas of the business. These sessions need to be short-ish (three hours or so maximum). You then give everyone an hour off, then send them back into their jobs...with the manager walking between them and coaching them as they work. 'That was great'; 'Remember to do this'; 'Have you checked that' – and so on.

This kind of training takes commitment because it's a big initial drain on managers' time (you can't do all the staff at once, so it can be tricky logistically). But it's worth it because it really **does work**. The key is that staff get the theory in the first session and the practical application *straight away* in the second. So what they learn is immediately reinforced by actually doing it in real live situations – i.e. in their normal jobs.

The other advantage is that the training is easy to refresh. Because it's done in small groups, it's not difficult to reconvene a group if people need a top-up.

Setting service firelighters

We've mentioned before that giving great service is infectious (see Chapter 3), and this is a very handy fact to remember when thinking of ways to help your staff keep climbing that service slope.

However big or small your organisation, you are sure to have a few natural service givers among your staff. And now you need to make the most of them!

People who are friendly and helpful, who always seem to know how to soothe a fretful customer or have time for a kind word, are really inspiring to others. And we've discovered that their effect can be doubled or even trebled by recognising and encouraging them in some public way. This doesn't necessarily have to mean extra pay or promotion, it can be as simple as appointing them 'service champion' for your store and giving them some training in coaching or extra customer service skills.

We think this is so effective for two reasons:

1. It gives your champion permission, and the confidence, to talk about and share their skills with their colleagues.

2. Other staff are happy to emulate them because this isn't some directive coming from 'the boss' – the champion is one of them, and if he/she can do it, so can they.

Being clear about who your key service givers are
This may sound obvious, but actually it's not. At the various Disney sites, for instance, they realised after some careful observation that in fact it was their cleaners who were the most important customer-facing staff of all. Why? Because they're the ones who the public are always approaching for directions/ information. So the Disney cleaners are given more customer service training than anyone else!

So you need to take a really close look at your organisation. Is it really the cashiers who need the most training, or would it be of more benefit to give those fellows pushing trolleys outside a good brush up?

WHAT TO DO ABOUT BEING TOO BUSY
We promised earlier that we'd talk about ways to deal with the 'being-too-busy-to-offer-brilliant-service' problem.

We've already discussed how adding the elements of brilliant service to the things that you already do takes no extra time at all. But there are also a couple of practical measures you can take to work smarter in the way that you deploy your staff.

The first is to **optimise your numbers** – i.e. to make sure you have more staff on duty during busy times and fewer when it's quieter. This might seem so obvious you wonder why we even mention it, but it's amazing (to us anyway) how many organisations don't do it. Call centres are absolute past masters at it – they've worked out in minute detail when their heaviest call volumes occur and have arranged staff shifts accordingly. But what if you're running a small furniture shop? You open at 9 a.m. but you know you almost never have a customer in before 10 – so why are all four of your staff in first thing? Wouldn't it be better to reserve your firepower for weekends and bank holidays? For supermarkets this is a real challenge – often your most experienced and older staff work 9 – 5 Monday to Friday and your youngest and least experienced work Friday evenings and Saturdays?

The second, less obvious measure, is **staff placement** – where you physically place your staff within your premises. When we worked with Eurostar, we found a big problem. Nearly all staff were positioned up by the ticket barriers, and then another member of staff by the gates, just before getting onto the train. This left huge blank spaces in between, with *no one* to ask for directions or information. In addition the lounges only held one train's worth of passengers, so if a train was delayed there was a huge back-up of people all trying to squash in together, with nobody to relay information or direct traffic. All we did was to appoint a 'master of flow', who was responsible for checking where problems were building up and moving staff around to deal with them. And the result was instantaneous: the whole service worked more smoothly; passengers were less frustrated and felt better served, and Eurostar staff were much happier as they didn't have to deal with nearly so many cross members of the public.

The banks too have recognised the value of placement. In many branches you enter these days there is someone sitting at a desk near the entrance, ready to ask customers what service they need and then directing them to (and helping them with) the automatic machines, the cashiers, the small business advisers or wherever. Queues have reduced dramatically, along with both staff and customer frustration. So it's well worth looking at the flow of customer traffic around your business to see if there are ways of strategically placing your staff to improve smooth running.

dangerous challenge

'REDUCING STAFF TO IMPROVE SERVICE'

What is the optimum number of staff to give the best service in your business and where should they be positioned? Try reducing the number of staff on duty but move them into new, greater customer contact positions – create your own master of flow or move a manager's desk into the store, reception etc., so that they can instantly be available for staff and customers.

ONE MORE THING

In all our travels among all our clients in all kinds of industries, there's one additional element we've noticed that can have a truly disproportionate effect on customers' perception of how well they've been served. And this secret is...?

The power of the unlikely suspect

If you listen to people talking about some fantastic experience they've had – a holiday, a meal, a shopping trip – you'll find that quite often it's been fantastic because some unexpected person was involved. 'The manager himself showed us round', they'll say; 'the captain came and sat at our table'; 'the dress designer was there herself to talk about her new line for the summer'. It happened to Phil and his wife when they had been for a particularly delicious meal at a restaurant in Dublin. 'The chef was quite a famous guy locally, and he came round all the tables himself after the meal to see how we'd enjoyed it,' Phil said. 'So not only did we have fabulous food, we also felt really privileged that he minded what we thought and had bothered to come out and enquire. It made it a truly memorable evening.'

Something like this has amazing power. The clue is in the way people say 'the manager *himself*', 'the Queen *herself*', 'the circus performers *themselves*'... The value lies in the fact that the key person, or people performing any activity have stepped outside of it to communicate directly with those on the receiving end. This makes them feel special and important – that they matter enough to the performer that he or she will come out of the charmed circle *just for them*.

The brilliant thing is that almost any business can use this power. Any hotel manager can spend half an hour having a drink in the bar, talking to the guests. The cabaret performers can be asked to come down to front-of-stage after their act. The potter who makes your best-selling mugs might be persuaded to chat to customers when in your shop. The only criteria to make this experience special is that it must be someone who's a) centrally involved and b) not normally to be expected by the customers.

AND FINALLY...
Beware the poo in the pool!

Picture the scene. You and all your fellow managers are at a conference in a nice hotel. You've finished the business for the day and are relaxing round the pool, cocktails in hand. 'Anyone for a swim?' someone cries. There's a general move to the pool... but there, floating in the water, are three horrible poos! There are cries of revulsion and the manager is fetched. No one's going in that water! The hotel manager is mortified. He's so sorry, he can't understand how it happened, he will call the pool operatives back in *right now*, they will work all night to empty the pool, they will scrub it and disinfect it...etc.

In the morning, before breakfast, you decide to start the day with a swim. The pool has been completely cleaned – you've just seen the pool operatives trailing tiredly past your window. So off you go with your towel. But there, bobbing cheekily around in the fresh water, is *another* poo! It's a different one from yesterday, smaller and a different colour, so it's definitely not that the manager and pool cleaners didn't do their work properly. Nevertheless, is there any way that you're going to dive in there? Like hell there is!

There are two points we're making here. The first is that poor staff, really bad ones, can have exactly the same effect as those poos. It doesn't matter how hard other people around them work, it still doesn't make up for the impact they have on customers. Their influence is far bigger than simply that of one individual. They affect everyone around them and spoil the efforts of colleagues, because customers remember the bad over the good. The second point is that even one poo can be just as bad as three. It's easy to think, 'Oh old so-and-so is a dreadful pain, but still – he's the only one and I'm used to dealing with him'. Yes, but what effect is he having, both on customers and on other staff, by being so painful? Be honest now!

So think carefully about your own staff. Is there a poo in the pool among them? And if so, is it really worth keeping them? In our humble opinion, they probably need flushing!

key learning points

- There are two big myths about creating fantastic customer service – that you need more staff, and that you need natural service givers. Rubbish! There are all kinds of things you can do with the staff you already have that won't stretch them or you to breaking point.
- Process is your best friend. If you design it carefully, it will automatically create the circumstances for brilliant service

to customers, even if the staff giving the service don't find that it comes easily. Build the magic into your routine!

- You do need to be explicit about how you want your staff to behave. This needs to be very simple and clear, but it must still give people the freedom to be themselves. Robotic service equals bad service to most modern consumers.

- The 'service plateau' – where people reach their comfort level and function on a merely adequate level – is the hidden enemy of really brilliant service.

- Action training, setting service firelighters and being sure who your key service providers really are are all effective ways of keeping up the energy and enthusiasm of your staff.

- The times when you really *are* too busy to offer fantastic service need to be minimised or eliminated. Optimising staff numbers and placing your people in the most strategic ways are the best ways of overcoming the problem.

- Try to harness the power of the unexpected wherever possible. It will delight your customers to an unprecedented degree.

- And finally – beware the poo in the pool. (And we'd be happy to bet that if you don't remember anything else about this chapter, you'll remember this section!)

chapter 6
signals of service

o, you've worked out how to gain your customers' loyalty; you've added the magic; you've segmented your customer base; you've brushed up your service leadership skills; you've turned all your staff into service heroes. What more can there be?

Look around you. Your atmosphere, your environment, that's what.

If you're going to be renowned for fabulous service, you need to achieve something pretty tricky. You need to get to a place where customers can come into your shop/restaurant/hotel/whatever and go out again saying, 'Wow, the service was fantastic!' *without* having exchanged one word with a member of your staff.

It is easy to forget that everything around you, every single thing customers and staff see, sends out an implicit signal about whether they are welcome, how much you care about detail, how committed you are to quality and so on. This is why we call them 'signals of service'. And all of them need to sing out to the world that you are about service, that this is a place of service. Get them right and your job is half done before you even encounter a customer face-to-face.

The only trouble is, because the message carried by these things is mainly subconscious, they can be quite difficult to spot. For instance, we visited a hotel recently and the first thing we saw in the car park was a big notice that said:

Attention!
Thieves operate in this area.
Management takes no responsibility for personal items left in your car.

Well, what of it? You often see this kind of sign. But what it's actually saying to hotel visitors (on a subconscious level) is:

> This is a disreputable area. We know it and you know it.
> You are likely to be robbed.
>   And if you are, don't come whining to us – it's your own
> fault.

Aargh! Is this really the kind of thing you want to say to your customers? There *must* be a way of warning people to be careful without making them feel that you don't give a damn.

As ever, though, we're here to help – so let's take a look at what we think is included in signals, and what isn't.

Signage – mind your language

This is one of the biggest issues. Signs are absolutely everywhere you look. Hotels, shops, restaurants, company reception areas etc. are full of them. In fact, they're so universal that much of the time we don't even notice them. But in terms of giving subliminal messages, it is essential to get them right.

There is an issue here that we need to warn you about right up front. Many companies we talk to immediately get what we mean, but then tell us that they are hampered by the organisation's 'brand police'. 'Everything we do has to look and sound a certain way', they say. 'We can't just write whatever we want, we have to reflect our corporate image in every detail, and that is set at executive level. All our signage is issued/vetted by our brand department; we do not have the autonomy to use humour in our signs!'

Of course, we do understand what they're saying. And yes, obviously, their messages do need to reflect their corporate look and feel. But we also believe that many brands have painted themselves into a corner that is too serious – that is to say too 'professional'. There is a real danger that those charged with looking after corporate image have become obsessed with formal protection, and that service suffers as a result.

What we would say is that 'branding' and 'service vision' are not the same thing. Signage is not about broadcasting a corporate message. It is about giving the person who reads it a feeling of being welcomed and served. So while it should *look* right in terms of reflecting company image, the *language* should be friendly, humorous, personal. Every sign is a message to an individual – and this is what should be kept in mind above and beyond anything else when it is being written. If it helps, show this chapter to your branding department next time you need to put up a new notice. It's worth emphasising that having a separate service vision doesn't detract from your brand – it enhances it!

> Dear Guest,
> We really hope you have a great stay with us. Please remember to bring all of your valuables into the hotel as we can't be responsible for things left in your car, but we are very happy to store things for you if needed.
> Thank you.

May be something like this sign may send a better signal of service with the same overall message.

One point to note: some companies have built their entire brands around being approachable/cuddly etc. (e.g. Innocent, Pret A Manger, Virgin), so friendly signage is not a problem for them. Don't be disheartened if you can't go as far as they do... just keep their example in mind!)

This notice on tables at Pret A Manger is a great example of a signal of service and a real reflection of the importance service and feedback is to them as an organisation – and written in a lovely friendly tone.

The Malmaison hotel 'do not disturb sign' makes something ordinary witty and amusing.

dangerous customer service

Innocent has created a whole movement (copied now by many) on how to do labelling for products in a unique and service-friendly way.

Environment

Just for once, in the present climate, we're not talking about the wider environment here, important though that is. We mean your premises...furniture, colours, carpets, amenities for your customers. What do you do that sings out, 'we're here to serve'? Your waiting room, for instance. Is it full of dog-eared old magazines and a dirge-like atmosphere? Is it obvious where customers can go to find out information they need? Are shabby chairs and gloomy curtains going to make them dread the attentions of the dentist even more? One of our poor colleagues feels marked forever by a recent experience of a funeral parlour. Bad enough having to go there in the first place, but the waiting room was full of tired fake flowers, a strong smell of air freshener, sample headstones on the walls and adjacent doors labelled 'Memorial Room' and 'Toilet' respectively left her feeling virtually hysterical!

The message, as ever, is to try to see things through your customers' eyes. Can they wipe their shoes when they come in? Is there anywhere for them to put dripping wet umbrellas? Are there enough seats, or do you almost always have several people standing while they wait to collect their prescriptions?

Another aspect to look at when considering environment is flow. Where are people coming in? What do they need? What will they be expecting from the experience? We talked in the last chapter about how banks have improved in this respect – having someone sitting near the entrance to direct traffic – and the same considerations apply whatever your business. In your restaurant, for instance, it is not a good idea to put a romantic table for two right by the toilet door. Neither should you be so keen to maximise custom that no-one can eat without bashing elbows with the people on the next table.

And environment signals don't just apply to what you might regard as your core areas. The car park, as we saw above, is a good example. Rip down those menacing signs, clear up any litter, place bins in strategic places and, if you *are* unfortunate enough to be located in a disreputable area, add a properly functioning barrier or good fence. Think too about what it looks like. A bed or tub of cheerful flowers can make a huge difference. And for goodness sake, if it's a busy car park, do **not** put the exit where it might impede the entrance. We know of a hospital where we suspect visitors from three weeks ago are still waiting to get out, thanks to the fact that cars trying to exit have to cross in front of those coming in!

In short, amending your atmosphere does not have to be expensive. It is simply a case of thinking about service when organising space – both in terms of logistics and how it looks and feels.

Uniforms

Uniforms, if done properly, are a physical sign to both staff and customers that helps to make great service inevitable. You don't just have to take our word for this – there's even been some research done that showed how cleaners who have been issued with uniforms do a better job than cleaners who have not!

So, what does 'done properly' mean? Two things, we'd say:

1. It is essential that uniforms are crisp and clean. Stained aprons and saggy old overalls are the stuff of horror movies...as soon as you see one, you know something horrible's going to happen! Novotel's slogan sums it up: 'Look professional, be professional'.

2. Uniforms must fit with your company image. (See, we're not going against brand identity – we're teaching you to complement it!). Asda is brilliant at this: its staff wear huge badges, sweatshirts etc., looking super friendly and not posh – the brand on legs, so to speak, so that staff are signals without even opening their mouths. Customers don't actually need to speak to them to feel that great service is in place.

Even if your brand is normally more formal, you can sometimes afford to 'play' a little. Grand old Selfridges, for instance, at Christmas issued its staff with 'Speak to me if you don't know what to buy' badges. These made people smile, as well as giving them permission to ask for help. And at Ibis hotels in Belgium, the staff name-badge is shaped as a smile.

Communications

By communications, we mean any way you use to reach out to a customer, whether it's letters, emails, faxes, text messages, flyers...even sky writing, if that's the kind of thing you do.

This is another area which can be blighted by the brand police, and you may not have any choice about printed items such as flyers and brochures. However, like signs, most forms of communication are messages received directly by one individual...the person reading them. So wherever possible, try to include a bit of yourself – especially in cases where your judgement tells you that the approved version is pretty poor. NHS outpatients' letters, for example, are terrible! (We're allowed to say this, as we're working with the NHS to improve matters.) They contain little information, no detail, no explanation and are often unintelligible to the non-medical. They also frequently contain photocopies, which look dreadful.

Note to self:
Do not under any circumstances use photocopies!

There is almost always a way to add a little personal touch, whatever the form of communication. For example, Phil recently booked an Ibis hotel in Calais online, and was surprised and pleased when he checked his inbox for the confirmation email. Instead of simply receiving a standard electronic response in that terrible font that we thought died out with the telex, the email 'appeared' to have been sent from the manager himself, stating that he would be delighted to welcome Phil on such and such a date, and signing it with his own name. It has stood out in Phil's mind, being so different from the norm. So if you *do* have to send out a vile brochure full of corporate speak, what's to stop you putting in a compliment slip with a nice personal message to take the sting out of it?

Websites are another medium where a perceived need for 'professionalism' can become a problem. But even the most professional-looking website can still flex to be service-oriented. Housing associations, for example, have a very varied customer base, from every different kind of individual you can think of to councils and corporations of every flavour. So in their case, consistency across their websites does not seem even appropriate...pages surely *ought* to feel and read differently, according to who is most likely to be reading them!

dangerous challenge

Don't ask Corporate Comms and fool them with a little smoke and mirrors.

What would happen if, instead of checking with all the right departments, you simply did what you knew to be the right thing for your customers?

We love corporate comms teams and work with them a lot but they are often much more interested in the look, layout, colour palette, correct logos etc. than in the words themselves. You can use this blind spot to your advantage! Make sure you obey every last rule on look and feel but use words that will appeal to your customers more than the usual approved corporate speak and you will probably get away with it!

Props for service

Lots of companies are doing these nowadays, and hooray for them we say. Examples are the McDonald's toys in children's food bags, colouring pencils and pads almost everywhere, coffee machines and/or water fountains in waiting areas... all the little extras that make customers feel loved and looked after. Some organisations worry about the cost – but really, how much can a plastic cup of water set them back? Especially when you set this against the goodwill generated. Another colleague of ours bought a pretty felt handbag for a little girl the other day, in a shop that had free lollipops for the children on the counter. As she was wrapping the bag, the shop assistant put four different coloured lollies into it. 'You can't give a handbag with nothing in it!' was how she put it. Result? Magic...again!

Do beware, however, that you don't let people think they're getting a little giveaway only then to find out that they are not. A certain bank we could mention had boxes of Thomas the Tank Engine badges on the cashiers' counters, looking for all the world as if they were there to give to small customers. Rage among mummies ran high when they discovered, too late, that they were then having several pounds deducted from the money handed to them by the cashier!

Staff facilities

We cannot emphasise strongly enough that service signals do not only speak to your customers. They are just as important for your staff. What we've already said about uniforms applies equally to staff facilities: staff who look smart and feel looked after are far more likely to put in the effort on the service front.

We discovered a perfect example of this in a rather surprising place. Habitat, for all the beauty of its product offering, is not known for brilliant service. But once we'd had a look behind the scenes, we were no longer surprised by this. Staffrooms and rest areas are furnished with all the broken, unsaleable, dirty, limp, tired cast-offs from the shops! No wonder the staff performance seems somewhat limp, tired etc. too...it is a reflection of what they see around them!

One factory inspector we know was so convinced of the link between how staff are treated and productivity/efficiency that he made a point of always using the staff toilets, particularly in the dirtiest and noisiest parts of the factory. 'In one place I visited, there weren't even doors on the cubicles, taken off by managers checking on staff spending too long in the toilet.' Unsurprisingly enough, the service ethos in that place was conspicuous by its absence!

Little extras

Besides the props for service that we mentioned above, there are all kinds of other little things you can do that say 'we didn't need to do this, but we did it because we care'. All it takes is a bit of imagination. Once again, examples are the best way of illustrating what we mean:

Virgin Windowgazer Guides are available on Virgin trains, and act as a free guide to what passengers can see out of their window during their train journey, including places of interest and brief histories etc.

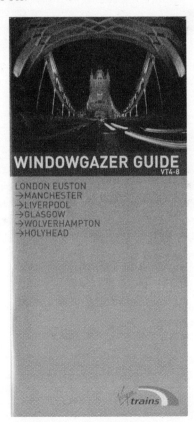

Below is an example of Haven Holidays' 'Report it and we will sort it' card, which is handed to all their guests on arrival, so that they have no worries about going back to reception, or about querying any small thing that might be wrong with their chalet.

Obviously what you do has to be relevant to your own business and your own customers, but these examples are enough to show you what *can* be done when careful thought has gone into what people might appreciate.

Five senses

When thinking about your service signals, it might help to consider them in terms of look, sound, smell, touch, taste, and feel. All five senses affect customers' overall sense of service. We've got just one example in mind when talking about this: St George's Hospital in London, which has recently spent £1 million on improvements...not to operating theatres, equipment or anything else, but to the entrance.

Outside the doors there is a garden, which has a big gravel area dotted about with little sitting areas, bamboo screens, and so on. People can sit peacefully, gathering their courage or just eating their lunch. Inside, all is marble and glass doors, with a **very** wide entrance and reception area. There's a shop, a café, a reception desk with all the reception staff in uniform. The point is that the whole approach gradually helps people get used to the idea of going into hospital – and by the time they get inside and past reception, their favourable first impressions are fixed. We've talked to patients, visitors and staff, and they *all* think it's great. Money well spent!

key learning points

- Signals of service are the things that show your customers you care, even if they never exchange a single word with you or your staff.
- Signs need to be friendly and speak to the individual reading them.
- Physical environment must be considered carefully, both in terms of logistics and look and feel.
- Uniforms create uniformity – of service and professionalism.
- Communications of all kinds can be personalised and still remain professional.
- Little giveaways are great, but never let a customer feel they're getting something for free if in fact they're not!
- Signals are for staff as well as customers. Their environment and facilities are just as important as those for the public.
- With a bit of imagination, little extras can create a magic of their own.
- Thinking about signals in terms of all five senses can help you to get them right.

chapter 7
training
your
customer

Training your *customer*? What weird revolutionary idea is this? But no modern book on service would be complete without considering the world we live in today. But let us remember the old world just for a moment; my parents used to drive into a petrol station, wind down the window and ask an attendant to 'fill her up please'; I used to pay money into my bank by handing it over to a person behind a glass screen; the highlight of my lunch-time supermarket experience used to be the idle chatter of a check-out assistant asking me if I needed help packing my sandwich and drink! But this is not the case now, in a world in which people do much of their shopping on the Internet, where self-service tills are popping up in every supermarket, and where finding a person behind a screen in a bank is a feat of detective work. This is the world of self-service. It is even self-service entertainment through Facebook, YouTube etc. A world, in other words, where it can actually be quite hard to be served by a person and where, consequently, a great many customers are serving themselves in all kinds of transactions.

So if customers are getting all independent and sorting themselves out, where do you and your service ethos come in?

Well, it's all to do with creating the right structure and providing the right direction. Get these right, and what you're doing is helping customers to help themselves to have a fantastic experience.

Clear? No? Better get down to some nitty-gritty then.

The fact is that even in an environment where the customer is creating their own experience – on Facebook, for instance, where the interaction between customers *is* the experience – the navigation has to be simple, clear and fun so they can find their way around; upload times have to be fast so that the whole experience can be fluent, spontaneous and match the Facebook brand; the website has to be extremely robust to withstand thousands of people using it simultaneously, and so on. *There* is your service element.

We think there are four areas that need to be included when considering this aspect of service:

1. Providing the right structure and direction.

2. Methods of managing your customers so that they have the experience you want them to have.

3. Using customers to raise and maintain the level of service.

4. Service between customers.

So, let's take these one at a time.

PROVIDING THE RIGHT STRUCTURE AND DIRECTION

We have talked a great deal through the rest of this book about people serving people. Now we need to talk about machines or things serving people and – crucially – training those people to be happy about it.

Self-service is an interesting issue. Obviously there are many commercial drivers behind its development – the main one being the fact that it is much less labour-intensive than traditional forms of service, and therefore much less expensive to provide. However, this is not the only reason for its rapid development. Ever since the invention of the first supermarkets in the United States in the early 1900s, self-service has been seen as a *positive* experience for the customer. Nobody knows exactly why it's been so popular: is it really so much better to go to a supermarket with a trolley, rather than into a shop with a list where all products are brought to you? Perhaps it's about choice – browsing and choosing your own apples at your own pace in your own time kind of thing. Perhaps it's about control, with the customer enjoying being in command of his or her own experience. Perhaps it's simply societal, with people now being much more used to doing things for themselves rather than relying upon others to serve them.

> # pauʃe for thought...
> Strangely enough, online shopping is actually re-introducing some of the old ways of shopping. The customer presents a list, and someone else picks the items and delivers them to the customer's home. Who'd have thought it...full circle or what?

Familiarity breeds content
Whatever the cause, there can be no doubt that a) people like self-service and b) the whole phenomenon continues to progress and become increasingly complex. From those first heady Piggly Wiggly days (yes, believe it or not, that is what the first supermarkets were called), customers have progressively got used to goods being displayed in categories, metal baskets, car parks, trolleys, barcodes, credit cards, electronic tills, and the whole supermarket experience. But none of those things happened overnight: each one was a slow development, gradually incorporated into the normal shopping experience, with customers acclimatising very gently to their use in each case.

And this is the important point. Customers need to be *trained* – subtly and unobtrusively – to accept innovation wherever it occurs.

The current big thing in retail stores, of course, is the self-service till. And this is the perfect example of what we're talking about. The very first self-service till appeared in New York in 1992...and yet only now, nearly 20 years later, are they being widely adopted. Sainsbury's first introduced scanner guns 10-15 years ago, where you scanned your own goods as you put them into your trolley then handed the scanner gun to a check-out assistant, who took your money without checking through all of your items. They then got rid of them again as people simply weren't ready to use them, although interestingly Waitrose have reintroduced them and they are now more popular.

We really do believe that this comes down to the customer training – i.e. familiarisation – involved. Two contrasting examples illustrate the point. Accor hotels tried a self-service check-in machine at one of their hotels in Reading. They struggled to get people to use it. Chiltern Railways, on the other hand, put in a self-service ticket machine at Warwick Parkway station, which has been a huge success. The difference is? Chiltern had someone standing by the machine for several months, educating passengers in how to use it. In fact they still man it in busy periods, and at peak times it's the staff member who operates it...and they do this *instead* of opening a second window in the ticket office. In this way, Chiltern is continually acclimatising passengers to the fact that the machine can be the fastest, most efficient way of purchasing a train ticket. They are continually training customers.

Can self-service ever be as good as personal service?

Most of us have an in-built feeling that no automatic or mechanical service can ever be as good as face-to-face service from a person. But is this true?

You only have to look at lists of which companies have been voted top for customer service to find your answer. The truth is that Internet companies are up there with the very best of the bricks and mortar store. Amazon, as we've said before, is regularly chosen as the customers' favourite among favourites, providing a truly superb service experience with no human interaction whatever. In fact, Amazon positively wants customers to manage *everything* themselves via the website. They do not want any of their staff, ever, to need to talk to a customer in person. This is absolutely the last resort, and if it ever does happen, they see it as a failure in their service.

So, a mechanical means of enabling people to serve themselves can actually be just as satisfying for customers as having a human being serving them...with the added advantage that a machine does not yawn, grunt, scratch or scowl at children. In addition, a machine is consistent in its treatment of all customers – it is not likely to favour women with babies over blokes on their own – and will be polite however annoying, or annoyed, the customer.

Is combining man and machine the ultimate service combo? In our local Tesco where now more than half of the checkouts are self-service there are normally one or sometimes two members of staff working in the area on hand, checking that everything is OK with customers using the machines. These members of staff are free to give great service to customers, often chatting with people as they move from machine to machine.

dangerous challenge

'GET RID OF ALL OF YOUR STAFF'

What if your business had no staff at all (or very, very few) how would you provide the kind of service experience that your customers would love? Spend a few minutes trying to justify each role in your organisation – could it not be done better by a machine? Now slowly introduce a few staff roles. What could they be doing to enhance the experience given by the machines?

In summary

From all these observations, there are a number of lessons we can extract about ways of enabling customers to help themselves:

- Even though a lot of customers are having their service experience with machines, it still needs to be great customer service.
- Providing for self-service should be about enhancing the service experience, not just cost-cutting. As long as customers trust the self-service process (i.e. they know how to use it and they believe it will do what they want), they will probably enjoy being in control.
- When designing self-service in a business, it needs to be step by step.
- When introducing self-service, businesses need to have people doing things alongside: customers need someone with them for a long time. For example, when introducing a machine, it needs to be manned. Schipol airport did this very successfully with its automatic check-in machines, keeping them staffed for several months before gradually reducing attendance as passengers got used to them.

How do you know whether self-service is right for your customers?

With all these thoughts in mind, the next question to ask is whether yours could be a self-service company. Our reply is that *all* companies could be, certainly in places.

Think about air travel, for example. Once upon a time, travelling was one of the most pampered and looked-after-by-other-people activities you could engage in. From buying your ticket to checking in, loading your luggage to receiving your meals, everything but everything was taken care of by airline staff. Look at it now though – especially if you're flying on a budget. You have to check in online before getting to the airport; you only go to the desk if you have luggage (and they'd prefer that you didn't); many of them don't provide meals, certainly on shorter flights; the hostesses who used to show you the emergency drill have been replaced by a tannoy and screens in the seats...we're just waiting for them to install drinks machines on board, and you'd never have to speak to anyone from the airline at all!

This description might make you wince a bit, but we're not necessarily saying that such streamlining is a bad thing. What these airlines have done is to take a very careful look at what they're about – their brand, in other words – and to automate accordingly. So their ethos is to be fast, cheap and no frills, and their automation has helped significantly to build that vision.

There are various lessons to be drawn from this. Ask yourself the following questions:

What is my brand?

What does your brand represent? Where are you on the service scale? Are you aiming to be Harrods, or Argos? If, say, you have a personal shopping business, you might decide that your brand is all about *you* – it's the individual one-to-one attention that forms the basis of your business, and that self-service for customers therefore doesn't come into it. McDonald's, for very different reasons, might also decide that self-service is not appropriate. There is a local McDonald's 'drive thru' that has developed an eye-wateringly speedy method of service. At the back of the building, you give your order to an assistant with a hand-held order machine; you drive round to one window at the front, where you hand over your money, then move to the next window where your food is passed out to you – usually absolutely immediately. The whole process only takes a couple of minutes. Customers serving themselves, in this instance, might actually muck it all up and compromise the essence of this particular service offer: speed!

At the opposite end of the scale, though, you might find that – Amazon-like – there are all kinds of aspects of your service that customers *could* do for themselves, and actually enhance their experience in the process.

pause for thought...

If you look back on Chapter 2 (Basics and Magic), you will remember that we said that your basics are your brand. And your basics are the things that every customer experiences every time, every day. We think that most organisations' basics are the things that could be suitable for automation. YO! Sushi, for example, has taken the basics of the restaurant industry – taking orders and serving food to customers – and made them self-service. A conveyor belt in the centre of the restaurant carries the dishes round and round and customers help themselves, having first looked up what the dishes are on the menu. No ordering, no waiting on tables, and customers love it – that feeling of being in control has become part of YO! Sushi's magic.

What kind of interactions do my customers have with my organisation?

To give you an example, Tesco's self-service tills are only suitable for customers with baskets: the counters are small and there isn't room to unload and scan an entire trolley-full. Waitrose, on the other hand, issues customers with hand-held scanners that they can carry around with them, enabling them to scan their whole weekly shop. Both supermarkets have considered the kinds of interaction their customers have with them, and made choices around those interactions.

That's what you need to do. If you were Starbucks, for instance, would you ever introduce self-service? And if you did, what elements would that include? Perhaps it might be only during the morning rush hour, when office workers in search of coffee could help themselves, quickly and easily. Or perhaps it could be just the most regularly ordered drinks...only the Americano, say.

It is all about segmenting the kinds of transaction you have with your customers and choosing which of those might be suitable for automation.

What is the difference between a transaction and a service moment?

These two things used to be very different: one was when the customer paid the service provider, the other was when the service provider helped the customer in some way. In some places now though, the boundary between the two is becoming blurred. In the big chain pubs, for example, when you go to the counter to order your food, the fellow behind the bar is likely to punch your request into a specialised till which has all the available options displayed on a screen. The till automatically tots up what you owe at the same time as creating an order – combining the transaction and the service moment, in other words.

We're wondering how long it will be before customers themselves are offered the machine, to punch in their own orders. You can just imagine it...the little touch pad at the end of your table, where you look at icons on the screen and press the ones you want, and it tells you how much the bill will come to. With only a small stretch, you can also imagine the machine informing you what today's specials are; how long you might need to wait, whether there are any delays in the kitchen, and so on and so forth. In some bars you can serve yourself drinks already by swiping with a credit card!

Once again, it is entirely possible that this kind of automation might actually enhance the customer experience rather than detracting from it. No more half-leaping out of your seat trying to catch a busy waiter's eye; no more fretting that your middle daughter *still* hasn't decided what she wants to eat when someone comes to take your order...

What other kinds of service do my customers experience?

This is about considering what other sorts of service your customers encounter on a regular basis – not just from your competitors, but in other spheres of their lives too. For instance, because the low-cost airlines have been such trailblazers in getting customers to do everything themselves, those customers are much more used to the idea of self-service than they used to be. As a result, the way has been paved for completely different organisations – nothing to do with travel at all – to introduce self-service elements too. In other words, consumers' expectations of service have changed over time, and there's no reason why you shouldn't take advantage of this in your own business.

pause for thought...

There is one thing you do need to be careful about though, and that is not alienating frightened users. Although customers are pretty technology-savvy on the whole now, many still are not, and you certainly don't want to scare them away. Even when you've made every provision for gradually training your customers in the use of your automated gizmo, your choices for self-service need to be about intelligent use of function. Don't supply any more than necessary, regardless of how clever you think something might be!

METHODS OF MANAGING YOUR CUSTOMERS

By this, we mean organising things in such a way that customers have the experience that you want them to have. A lot of this we covered in the chapter on signals of service. For instance, the way you manage queues will mean that either customers have a long boring wait or the queue moves quickly and they get to a service point with a minimum of trouble. You get to choose which experience you'd prefer them to have.

But managing customers is about more than service signals – it's about creating a whole experience. IKEA is an interesting example of this, in that its entire design is based around leading customers from one room-set to another – experiencing all the company's products in situ, so to speak. This was particularly brilliant when IKEA first came on the scene in the eighties – no one had ever seen anything like it before. But in these days of personal choice and direction, it can seem rather too rigid. The fact that you *have* to go round in a snake of people, experiencing the store in the order that IKEA says you must, now seems a tad dictatorial. Being the savvy company that it is, though, IKEA has taken note of this, introducing 'shortcuts' in its stores so that independently-minded customers can deviate from the route set.

Supermarkets too are another example worth noting in the way they manage customers. They are very clever in the way they pipe enticing smells over the doorways, to make people hungry as they come in, and move products around frequently so that even regulars walk past new items at each visit.

And the instance we quoted elsewhere of the National Trust and other attractions compelling visitors to leave via their shops, is another shrewd management technique. With a little imagination, this last option can be taken even further. If you were running a zoo, say, wouldn't it be even more attractive to customers (not to mention your bottom line) to have a stand selling cuddly monkeys *by* the monkey house, and not just in the shop at the end? Ditto for penguins/crocodiles/creepy crawlies/ all other species you have in the zoo?

Some quick suggestions
Here are a few more examples that we've seen about the place, that might prompt your own ideas on customer management.

Make your self-service options attractive – In Tesco, they try to make sure that the queues at the normal check-outs are longer than on the self-service tills, making it attractive for customers to serve themselves. Halifax in Leamington has all its self-service machines at the front and its manned desks right at the back, so customers have to be determined to get to them!

Provide plenty of information – In the lifts of one hotel, we found 'traffic light' posters showing the peak times for breakfast in the restaurant. The red light period, from 7.00-8.00 a.m., was when it was busiest (and waiting times were longest). Business guests in a hurry could therefore opt to go earlier; holiday guests could choose to go later and eat in peace. Motorway signs have adopted a similar philosophy: they now flash up how many miles it is to major junctions, and how many minutes it should take to get there. Motorists can thus make their own decisions about whether to take evasive action, should there be delays. Alton Towers and Disneyland do the same thing: screens at regular intervals along the queues tell visitors how long they can expect to wait before reaching the attractions. Once again, people can choose for themselves whether or not to hang on that long.

USING CUSTOMERS TO RAISE AND MAINTAIN THE LEVEL OF SERVICE

The promise you make – the whole brand ethos that you create – sets an understanding among customers about exactly what it is they can expect to receive from you. If you're the Body Shop, for instance, they will 'know' that your products are natural, ethically sourced, not tested on animals etc. If you're Virgin, they will think funky, innovative, giving-established-giants-a-run-for-their-money and so on.

If, however, you then fall down on some aspect of that promise, all hell will be let loose. Imagine if a John Lewis store manager lost his temper and slapped a customer: all of middle England would rise in protest! We talked in Chapter 1 about how M&S had slipped up with its online ordering over one Christmas and delivered items late or not at all. That made the front pages of the national press. Outrage – this is not what we expect from the nation's favourite store!

The point we're making here is that the promise you make to customers, whatever it is, *trains* them to expect a certain level of service. And if they don't then get it, it causes huge kickback. By making your promise very explicit, in other words, you are actually turning your customer into your quality assurance.

SERVICE BETWEEN CUSTOMERS

This isn't so much about training your customers as about discovering what customers are saying about you to each other. For instance, one consultant we know from the Birmingham Children's Hospital said that Facebook was the place where patients and families were exchanging information about their experiences. No one was using the official websites provided by the NHS.

In the same way, people are using chat-rooms and blogs to find out how to mend their cars, how to operate software on their computers, how to swap their TVs over to digital, etc. More and more it is consumers, rather than providers, who are helping each other to make the most of products and services.

The reason why you, as a service provider, need to be aware of this trend is that it has immense power. Very few people will fill in your carefully structured 'Satisfaction Survey' or 'Customer Feedback' form, but they will happily chat to each other about what is good and bad about your service. If you want to know what's really going on and how you can improve what you're offering, you need to tap into this bush telegraph.

key learning points

- In these days of automation and customers serving themselves, it is not quite so obvious where your own service element, as the provider, comes in. However, it is just as important as ever, only in slightly different forms:

  - *structure*: the method that customers use to self-serve must be robust and appropriate;
  - *training*: you need to acclimatise customers gently to using self-service mechanisms.

- Customers *like* self-service...they always have, ever since it first came into being. It can be just as satisfying as personal service, and people are getting more and more used to it.

- Almost every organisation could make parts of its offer self-service. When considering which parts, think carefully about your brand and your basics. Any automation must enhance your brand and not detract from it, and your basics are the most likely things to lend themselves to being automated.

- As part of training your customers to use and enjoy self-service, consider ways of managing their journey through your shop/website/theme park/whatever, to ensure that they have the experience you want them to have.

- Make your promise to customers, whatever it is, very explicit so that they know what to expect from you. If you then get a strong reaction because that expectation is not being fulfilled, you know you are falling down on the job.

- Find out how your customers are communicating with each other and what they are saying about you. It's the best possible way of hearing the truth, and therefore a valuable means of improving your service offering.

chapter 8
rewards
and
recognition

If you say the word 'reward', what is generally the first thing that pops into your head? That's right – money. All those 'wanted' posters with pictures of evil-looking criminals and promises of large amounts of cash for bringing them in. And when organisations talk about 'rewards' (which they do a lot), they also tend to mean money...some sort of special payment for particular kinds of performance.

Throughout this book we have talked a lot about your staff – training them, motivating them, helping, understanding and developing them, all in the interests of creating fantastic service for your customers. They are absolutely central to your business and yes, it is therefore important to reward their efforts and recognise their achievements. However, we do not think that money is actually either sustainable or appropriate as a means to reward service (or anything, really). In fact, this is a cash-free chapter. If you are looking for advice on a financial incentive scheme of some kind, it probably isn't for you.

So, rewards and recognition. What *do* we mean by them? Why do you need them, and how are they different from each other?

A COUPLE OF QUICK DEFINITIONS

A **reward** is not a performance bonus, it is not about getting tips for things. It is a gift that is of value, but not monetary. It is a formal, tangible present from an organisation to an individual to thank them for their efforts. The tangibility bit, having something that can be held in the hand, is important. The employee can take it home, show people, talk about it, put it on their mantelpiece. Even more important, we think, is that it should be *shareable*. If it's a voucher for a meal out, say, or a nice bottle of wine, another person gets drawn into it too. The recipient can take her husband out to the meal, share the bottle with his friend, or whatever. This joint effect at least doubles the impact of the reward. After all, almost everyone enjoys showing off – just a little bit – when they've done well.

Recognition is the fanfare that goes with the reward, and is about the people side of the formal gift. It is about the individuals around an employee noticing and appreciating what they do, and saying so publically. It's the 'public' bit here that is vital. If you, an employee, receive a nice present for being so good at your job, that's all fine and dandy. But if no one else knows you've been given it, or why, it loses its impact considerably.

You need both, in other words. Rewards and recognition go hand in hand.

WHAT SHOULD R&R BE FOR THEN - OR NOT FOR?

This is where it gets complicated, so pay attention. Virtually all organisations of any size have R&R schemes, but far too many of them are not thought through properly. We read of one local authority, for instance, which gave rewards to staff who *didn't* go off sick. What sort of a message did they think that sent, for goodness sake? 'We think you're all actually a bunch of lead-swingers, so anyone who can be bothered to turn up is special'?! Were their expectations of staff really so low?

When designing a reward scheme, you need to give careful consideration to a number of factors.

1. Complexity

This is not to be under-estimated. What are you rewarding, exactly? Should it be the basics of service, or just the magic? Are rewards for those who follow rules, or for those who break them and use their own initiative?

In other words, do you give the prize to the person who gives consistently good service all day every day, or to the one who does something extraordinarily wonderful once, but who is usually a grumpy sod? If you think both should be rewarded, do they get the same reward or different ones? And what about the people behind the scenes – the washer-uppers in the restaurant, or the warehouse staff in the supermarket. They don't encounter customers, but shouldn't they have a chance to receive rewards too? If so, what kind and what for?

2. Defining your criteria

It is not very useful simply to have vague ideas about rewarding staff for 'good service' or 'doing their job well'. What do these mean? Everyone, managers and staff, needs to know exactly what is being looked for. This comes back to what your business is actually *about*. In the private sector, for example, the fundamental purpose of any business is to make money. You might decide, therefore, that that is what you will reward: the waitress who serves so well in your restaurant that customers buy extra bottles of wine; the assistant in your shop who manages to sell shirt, tie and cufflinks to go with the suit. Up-selling then, in this case, is your criterion for reward. Or perhaps it might be for creating loyalty. Someone in your hotel provides such wonderful service to a guest that he and his family return again and again. Or it might be for quality: your despatch team reduces errors in delivery by a margin of X per cent. Whatever it is, it needs to be clearly defined and spelled out.

3. Frequency

Should your rewards be given daily? Monthly? Annually? Maybe you should have an 'employee of the week' prize, awarded on Fridays. It all depends on what you think might be most motivating for your particular staff. With a sales team, for instance, might it keep everyone's energy up if you had some sort of daily mini-announcement? Or should you go for smaller rewards on a monthly basis, with one whopping jamboree for an overall winner at the end of the year?

4. Fairness

It is vital that all members of staff have equal opportunity to earn rewards. Anyone who doesn't feel 'in the loop' or that rewards might apply to them will feel positively disenfranchised. In fact it is much better not to have a reward scheme at all than to have one which makes staff feel that 'some people are more equal than others', to quote *Animal Farm*.

pause for thought...

We saw an interesting experiment in a school recently called 'the secret student'. Every day, it involved nominating one pupil out of a class full of teenagers as that day's 'secret student'. Teachers knew who'd been nominated, but the pupils themselves did not. For each lesson in which the chosen pupil behaved really well, they received a tick. Three ticks in a day gained a point for the whole class, the idea being that if they received enough points over a certain period, they would all be taken on a special trip to Alton Towers.

The clever part was that, because students knew the scheme was in place, they all encouraged each other to behave well each day. And because the emphasis was on positive reinforcement, they were only told who the secret student was when that person gained them a point. The experiment had remarkable results. Thanks to the mutual peer pressure, class behaviour improved beyond all recognition and the group made it to Alton Towers.

While we're not suggesting for a minute that staff should be treated like schoolchildren, there is some scope perhaps for using the power of peer pressure to up the game with regards to performance?

DESIGNING YOUR R&R SCHEME

So with all this in mind, where do you start if you want to design an R&R scheme?

Firm foundation

As often in this book, we'd recommend that you go right back to your grass roots/sea level/origins/call it what you will. Define, again, exactly what experience you want your client/patient/ customer to have. Enumerate all the elements that you and your staff provide that create that experience. And there you have it – a starter list of things to reward. The important point is that you need to create an unbreakable link between the rewards you offer and the service you provide. Ibis hotels, for example, identified five key behaviours that they believed created the ideal customer experience, and rewarded staff for demonstrating those behaviours. Doing something like this takes you down the route of rewarding the consistent delivery of basics and gives you a good firm backbone to structure the rest of your R&R policy around. It also means that you encompass the fairness issue we mentioned before. If, for example, you're in the hotel business and you identify 'friendly face-to-face encounters', 'spotlessly clean rooms', 'beautiful gardens' and 'excellent cuisine' as the things you want customers to experience, you automatically include everyone who provides those things, whether they're in customer-facing roles or not. Maintenance, cleaners and kitchen staff will be equally as involved as receptionists, waiters and bar staff.

You can further balance who receives rewards by widening the assessment criteria. In the case of Ibis hotels its Employee of the Month was based on three elements: 1) guest comments; 2) staff nominations, and 3) management discretion. Again this helps to ensure that it is not only the customer-facing roles such as receptionist or waiter, but also the admin support and the housekeeping, who are in line for recognition.

Once you've established *what* you want to reward on a regular basis and how you're going to select *who* receives those awards, you can then devise your regular rewards mechanism. Will it be employee of the month, or of the week? Will winners be in categories (like the Oscars), or will there just be one overall winner (like the Turner Prize)? Whatever form it takes, it needs to become regular and consistent and gain familiarity among staff... something that they know they will have a good chance of obtaining if they set their minds to doing so.

pause for thought...

TEAM REWARDS VERSUS INDIVIDUAL REWARDS

Team rewards are a special case when considering the who. There's been a sizeable shift towards more team-based awards in recent times but, when it comes to customer service, we're not sure if this is right. The outcome of team performance is rewardable – the delicious meal, the new product design, the new building built – but actual service is almost always one-to-one. Consequently, we feel that rewards for excellent service should generally be individual. You might need a combination of rewards.

The same applies when it's customers who are doing the rewarding – in the case of tips in particular. Many restaurants and other hostelries virtually oblige customers to hand over a universal tip to all staff by adding a service charge (10 per cent or so) to the bill. But what if a customer thought your maître d' was a grumpy old bat and the serving staff were great... shouldn't they be allowed to reward at their own discretion?

Magic moments

So the main structure is now in place. However, it is more than likely that this will not be flexible enough to cover all eventualities. Tesco, for instance, had a scheme called the 'Value Awards' which consisted of ten values ('no one works harder for customers' was one) that staff could be nominated for demonstrating. Great scheme, and covered almost everything. However managers still found themselves perplexed when faced with situations like the one in Chapter 2... you remember the lady who let the little blind girl sit on her lap at the till? Not only did this example not really seem to fit properly under any of the ten values, but neither did managers want to set it as precedent by rewarding it under the formal scheme.

We encountered an even more amazing example when we were working with Eurostar, that has since become legend throughout the company. A woman turned up at the ticket office, absolutely frantic with worry: her father had been rushed into hospital over in France, and she had to get there as fast as possible. There was a problem though – her friend had asked her to look after his pet duck for the weekend, and she'd had no time to arrange alternative duck accommodation. Indeed, there *was* the duck, under her arm. So perhaps Eurostar could see their way to allowing the duck to travel with her? Well no, obviously they couldn't, of course not. Oh dear – impasse. All was resolved, however, by the fabulous lady behind the desk. 'Not to worry madam,' she said, '*I'll* look after the duck.' And so she did, together with the rest of the booking office team, keeping the duck for 2 days in the back office.

Again, Eurostar would hardly want to establish such a thing as a precedent – ducks under desks not necessarily being conducive to concentration. Nevertheless, like the Tesco example, it was a fantastic piece of customer service and therefore couldn't be simply ignored...so what to do?

The answer is that your R&R scheme needs to contain some extra capacity to reward initiative rather than specific action. You need a looser 'spirit of the moment' type of reward, and managers and team leaders need to be given the freedom to bestow such an award at their own discretion. You could call it the 'Above and Beyond Award', or the 'Flash of Inspiration Prize', or the 'Outside of the Box Medal', or the... you get the idea. The point is that it needs to be clear that this reward is not a regular, mainstream reward – it is a special stand-alone one that is given for spontaneous or extraordinary moments of magic service.

Special circumstances

There's one more element to consider. Many organisations have particular times for promoting a specific product or service – Shell might devote a couple of months to increasing take-up of its loyalty cards in petrol stations, for instance, or a pub might be focusing on selling a guest beer over more regular ones. If this kind of thing applies to your organisation, you can't reward success within your regular R&R scheme; you need a specific and separate way of applauding those who perform best. The bar person who shifts the most of the special brew could be 'King/ Queen of the Speckled Gloucestershire Old Peculiar' (replace as appropriate) and receive a nice – non-financial – prize of some sort. Because the award is outside of your regular scheme, people tend to feel that if they make a special effort, they have a good chance of winning... even if they have no interest in aspiring to one of your normal rewards.

HOW TO DELIVER R&R

How you present the rewards is also important – it is after all the recognition part of the policy, which carries just as much weight.

It sometimes happens that, because rewards are a regular occurrence within an organisation, the recognition part becomes mundane – sort of corporate 'white noise'. But this is disastrous. Just because something happens frequently or regularly does not mean that it shouldn't still be special. People look forward to awards ceremonies, even little weekly or daily ones – and those who receive the rewards need to feel duly fêted. If they don't, there is little point in holding any kind of ceremony at all. Consequently, it is vital that proper attention is given to making even the tiniest of recognition occasions truly celebratory in nature... *every* time. **It matters** – and not just to the 'rewardee'. When other people share in a ceremony, there is a feel-good factor that not only creates a warm 'yes, that person deserves that reward' atmosphere but also encourages others to aspire to gaining rewards themselves.

Who you choose to present the reward is also important, particularly when that reward is for providing fantastic customer service. Because service is personal, by its very nature, the recognition part also needs to be personal. Say you work as an agent in a call centre. It has been tough. The bank you work for has cut the interest rates it's paying on savings and customers are not happy. They are phoning in droves to complain. You have dealt with one demanding call after another, remaining calm, sympathetic, kind and efficient day after day. When, after weeks of this, you are nominated to receive a reward for your wonderful service, the most effective way of receiving this is if *your* boss – who knows exactly what you've been through – is the one to smile into your eyes and say 'Well done, I'm proud of you'. It's nice that Ms Big Cheese, the manager of the entire call centre, is also there clapping heartily on the sidelines, but it's the personal commendation from someone who knows you well that means the most to you.

This point applies even when the ceremony is on a large scale – the special, annual, one-off National Employee of the Year jamboree, say. While yes, it is important that the Chief Executive and other Big Guns are there and are seen to be supporting and approving of the whole affair, it is still our opinion that the best person actually to present a reward to an employee is that employee's own boss. Best of all is if the Top Boss says something nice then hands over to the Personal Boss to make the award and give the heartfelt thanks.

MORE ON COMPLEXITY

We talked a little about this earlier, and it's when organisations underestimate just how complex rewards can be that some of the greatest difficulties can occur. Because all organisations are different and rewards that are appropriate for one may be totally unsuitable for another, we cannot provide a definitive list of dos and don'ts here. However, here are a couple of points that need careful consideration in order to navigate safely through potentially very choppy waters.

What to give to whom – Say you've decided that a jolly to Dubai for the weekend is a good reward for your most deserving employees. But among those employees are Angela, your top saleswoman; Keith from accounts who has not made one mistake in the payroll for 20 years, and Tilly from the ticket office who is sometimes a little inefficient but who made one customer luminously happy by rescuing her toddler from falling under a train. Is it appropriate that these three very different employees receive the same reward? The important thing is whether they think this is fair. If they don't, they are liable not only to hate each other, but also to hate you – for making the mistake. And the lovely reward will not be lovely any more, but a source of bitterness and recrimination. Don't scoff... we've seen this kind of thing happen, more than once!

To outsource or not to outsource – Many companies outsource their rewards to companies like Red Letter Days, who provide a wide range of different days out from hot-air ballooning to Formula One race days. This seems like a great idea – giving a voucher seems like a simple way to recognise someone's efforts, and they can then choose their own treat. So far, so good. Two issues arise, though. 1) Should there be a choice? Doesn't that take away the element of surprise? A gift that a person chooses themselves can lack the specialness of a gift that is chosen for him or her. 2) It is vital not to throw the baby out with the bath water. Outsourcing the reward part is one thing, but the whole recognition process must remain internal. Unless the latter is embedded as a regular part of the company ethos, there is very little point in providing the former.

dangerous challenge

WHAT WOULD HAPPEN IF...

... you got rid of rewards altogether? Could you train your managers so well that their management skills alone were enough to motivate the rest of the workforce?

... you handed over the design of your company R&R policy to the staff themselves? How about setting a budget, forming a working party and leaving it to them to come up with a scheme to suit your organisation?

AND FINALLY...THE SIMPLEST AND MOST EFFECTIVE REWARD OF ALL!

If all of the complexity of reward and recognition is too much and you are completely baffled to the point of not bothering at all then all you actually need to do is one thing. And that is to say thank you...and mean it.

Time and time again when we are working with organisations on their R&R schemes for customer service, when you ask their staff what is the one thing that would motivate them most, the thing they want more than anything else is more thank yous for a job well. A thank you at the end of a busy shift, a manager who comes around the following day and personally says thank you for the work done by the night team, a quiet word and pat on the back after a member of staff has dealt with a difficult customer. Remember the chapter on service leadership – the one-second positive coach – this is the basics and the starting place for your R&R scheme.

key learning points

- A reward should not mean money. It is a gift that has a value which is more than monetary... a gift of appreciation for someone's hard work. Making a reward something that can be shared – a meal out, theatre tickets – doubles its impact.
- Recognition is the public applause which goes with receiving the gift. Reward without recognition loses its impact considerably. Being given a nice gift for your efforts is not nearly so good if no one else knows about it!
- Most organisations of any size have R&R schemes, but many are not thought through properly and can actually have a detrimental effect on people's motivation and happiness. The four areas which need careful consideration are: complexity, criteria, frequency and fairness.
- Good R&R schemes should be based first and foremost on the consistent delivery of basics. Define exactly what you want your customers to experience, identify what elements contribute to them receiving that experience, and reward the people who provide those elements really well.
- Flexibility is also required. 'Normal' rewards won't usually fit extraordinary moments of magic service, so you need the ability to give 'special' rewards where they've been earned.
- Any work that falls outside of the regular, day-to-day business of your company – such as promotions of particular products or a focused drive to acquire new customers – needs its own specific rewards.
- When it comes to presenting rewards, the recognition part of R&R, there are two vital elements: making the presentation special and celebratory *every time*, and the personal touch.
- Particular dangers lie in what rewards you give to whom. The only way to steer clear of trouble is to make your R&R scheme as transparent as possible so everyone knows exactly what they can expect to receive if they perform to a certain level.

- Please don't forget the thank you. An R&R scheme, however good, does not replace those two little words.

chapter 9
service across cultures

This chapter may seem to be a sudden sidestep from the flow of the book so far, which has been a whistle-stop tour around helping you put in place the practical stuff to get great service happening in your organisation. However, we felt that no book on customer service in this day and age would be complete without talking about culture and the challenges and opportunities that this presents for delivering great customer service.

There's no getting around this one: culture is a tricky issue. Since this is, after all, a 'dangerous' book, we will come straight out with the dangerous statement that *everyone* is influenced by their culture. Learning to embrace and celebrate difference has probably always been the one thing that would most improve the lot of humanity. But now it's becoming increasingly urgent – particularly for anyone aiming to provide wonderful customer service (you, in other words!).

MULTICULTURALISM IS GETTING WIDER AND DEEPER, FASTER THAN EVER BEFORE

We've been talking about 'globalisation' for years and our countries have gradually become more multicultural. Recently though, this process has got faster, as well as more diverse. For example, from our personal experience of working with a hotel chain, in the course of one year, we found that the make-up of staff working for hotels in England changed drastically, from around 70 per cent British and 30 per cent European (mostly Spanish, French etc.) to 70 per cent European and 30 per cent British. In addition, these Europeans were now from Poland, Lithuania, Latvia, Moldova, Romania and so on. This picture is reflected across Britain's service industries, with nationals from every country of the world living and working here and contributing to our economy. And hooray, we say... a multicultural world is an infinitely richer, more interesting world.

However, a richer world is also a more complex one, and this can cause its own problems. One supermarket chain we know for instance, found this out the hard way when trouble erupted between its warehouse staff and its drivers. The drivers, mostly eastern Europeans, were arriving at warehouses and starting to unpack the lorries themselves, rather than sitting around waiting for the warehouse staff to do it. In their culture, if something needs doing, you just get on and do it. However, this didn't go down well with the warehouse staff, or the British drivers who saw it as either threatening their jobs or potentially more work for them to do. There was an awful row, which almost led to a strike, averted only by clear lines being drawn in the sand delineating who was to do what.

An equal, but opposite, problem arose in the care home where Phil's mother lives. Some of the new senior staff nurses had recently come from India, being highly qualified, and were happy to supervise the dispensing of drugs, advise on treatments and so on, but would not bathe the clients or put them to bed, even when other staff were run off their feet. 'I'm the nurse and those are care assistant duties,' was how one woman put it. Not her job. And you can see this. In India, every person has their own specific task, and they do not presume to intrude on other people's jobs. The shop-door opening man would not dream of stacking the shelves...that would be to take away the shelf-stacking man's employment. It's all about culture.

WHO DOES IT AFFECT?

Some kinds of business, obviously, are more exposed to different cultures than others. Tourism and travel, of course, are the first to come to mind. If your business is small or situated in some quiet rural backwater, on the other hand, it is tempting to believe that the issue of culture is not one that you need to think about. But you shop in supermarkets, don't you, where staff probably come from many different countries? You must have experienced phoning a call centre, which is likely to be situated offshore. Your local hospital is likely to employ doctors and nurses from all over the world. Your nearest petrol station may, like ours, be mainly run by Polish and Iranian students earning their way through their degrees. And in the pubs and restaurants around you, have you noticed that nearly all the waiters and waitresses seem to be beautiful young South Africans and Kiwis?

Whether you employ staff, serve customers or are simply yourself a customer, you are going to encounter a multitude of different nationalities. The issue of culture is one that affects all of us.

TREATING DIFFERENT CULTURES DIFFERENTLY

Businesses, of course, are already hyper-aware of this fact and, to be fair, have been making great efforts to adapt.

The idea seems to be that you must be culturally appropriate to every single person you encounter. There are hosts of books and websites on how to do business without causing offence in Japan; about what constitutes good manners in China; about what signals agreement in Russia, or in India. The bank HSBC appears to be making a major USP out of its cultural sensitiveness, as illustrated in its beautiful adverts about being 'the World's Local Bank'. They do not cause offence by using the wrong hand signals in Brazil. They save the faces of their Japanese clients by buying them expensive gifts after beating them at golf. This is all well and good for HSBC.

But in our experience there has been very little said, written down or researched on how you handle a multitude of different cultures all at the same time. Say you are someone from Poland, working in Britain for a French organisation, serving someone from China. How do you manage? Which culture should you be being sensitive to? Your own? Your employer's? Your customer's? Your host country's? It's almost impossible. And what about in a hotel...you might be a young Dutch receptionist welcoming a

British stag party, an elderly Spanish couple, a group of Japanese businessmen and an Indian family, all within the space of ten minutes. As that receptionist's boss, do you really teach her who to bow to (and how low), who to kiss (and how many times), whose hand to shake (and how hard), who to salute (and how high)?

We don't think so. It's hard enough to get a Brit in the UK to serve another Brit in the UK – or at least to do it really well!

But culture is extremely important, and fundamental to who people are. You can't just ignore it. So what *can* you do?

FACE THE FACTS

The first thing to do, we think, is to acknowledge that cultural is an issue. People don't talk about it, it's too sensitive. They are afraid of being branded as prejudiced or racist, of being publically shamed or embarrassingly reported in the press. But there are some facts, as listed below, that simply have to be recognised. Beneath each fact, we have suggested strategies – tried and tested by us – which can be very helpful in modifying them.

fact:

We all have a tendency to judge immediately on first impressions. If a guest coming in to your hotel approaches the desk and says, 'I want a room now!', there are few native English speakers who wouldn't see this as an order rather than a request and bristle in response. It would not occur to us that actually, there may be no word for 'please' in that guest's own language. Swahili is one such language; Icelandic another; Danish another.

What you can do?: We have already talked a little about our natural tendency to make assumptions about who people are, based simply on their appearance (see the Jimmy/Catherine exercise in Chapter 3). The emphasis here though is that, having made an instant judgement, there is then an instant decision to dismiss. 'I don't like the look of that person; I'm not going to bother with him/her' kind of thing.

Below is a brief exercise that is great for demonstrating to people exactly how quick their brains are to seize on a piece of information and react in a negative fashion. Try it with your team.

exercise

HOW WILL YOU GREET THEM?

Tell the group you are going to describe three people to them who are shortly going to be their customers. If you are in the hotel business, say that these people will be coming as guests; if you're a hairdresser, say that they will require styling...whatever is appropriate to your particular kind of business. Ask everyone to note how they feel about the prospect of dealing with each person. The three are:

- A black African terrorist, responsible for many deaths, who was imprisoned for many years and never offered any apology for his actions.
- An Indian sage who kept a strict vegetarian diet, held extremely contentious political views and travelled everywhere with a vast entourage of people.
- A rich white playboy, who inherited his money rather than earning it and was unfaithful to his wife right from early on in their marriage, causing a major scandal.

Ask for feedback on their reactions. If the group is typical of ones we've encountered, these will probably be somewhat negative.

Then say that this is actually rather strange. By and large, most people would feel it was an honour to sell a suit to Nelson Mandela/bring a drink to Mahatma Gandhi/service Prince Charles's car!

The message from this exercise is that it is perfectly natural to experience an immediate initial reaction. The important thing, however, is the action that follows the reaction. While the reaction may be beyond conscious control, how the person then chooses to *behave* is crucial. It is perfectly possible – and extremely important – to move from the automatic judge/dismiss response to a demonstration of interest/care. After all, isn't everyone at least curious to meet these three extraordinary customers?!

fact:

People working in their own countries sometimes feel that visitors should automatically conform to the cultural norms of that country. One of the worst examples we saw was in a hotel in Holland, when a large group of Chinese guests came into the dining room for breakfast. They obviously didn't realise that they were supposed to return their trays of used plates and cups onto a purpose-built rack after eating, and simply got up to leave once they had finished. One of the breakfast staff, however, was outraged and shrieked across the entire room that in this country they were expected to tidy up after themselves! You could have heard a pin drop – those poor guests.

What you can do?: Regarding the attitude that visitors to your country should conform to your ways, one of the best ways of modifying this is to show people firstly how strange those visitors may feel in alien surroundings, and secondly, how difficult they themselves might find it to conform to the visitors' nations. Here's another good exercise to get their minds working.

exercise

HOW WOULD YOU COPE?

Lay a long rope, 10 metres or so, out on the floor and divide it into ten (i.e. by marking it at one-metre intervals with coloured tape, or similar). Write all the different countries you can think of on individual pieces of paper, remembering to include the countries of customers to your business. Then get your team to place the pieces of paper along the rope wherever they think is appropriate in terms of cultural difference to your country (1 is very similar; 10 is very different). They need to consider factors such as climate, dress, behaviour, food, religion and anything else you think relevant when making their decisions. An English family on holiday in England, for example, would sit at zero, perhaps; German or French visitors might be placed at 1 or 2. Eastern Europeans or Scandinavians might come somewhere in the middle; a New Zealander or American might go at 6 or 7; a Ghanaian could rate an 8 or 9; a Chinese customer might sit at 10.

Once all the pieces of paper have been placed, then ask the group to consider how well they themselves might fit in when visiting each of the countries discussed, again considering the climate, dress, religion etc. Do they know, for example, that it is considered rude to sit with your feet pointing at anyone in Buddhist and Hindu countries? Do they know which of your samples *are* Buddhist or Hindu countries? In Malaysia, it is very impolite to point with your index finger – you're meant to hold your fist sideways, thumb on top, and point with your thumb. You need to be careful though: in Bangladesh, a 'thumbs-up' gesture is obscene!

This exercise, in other words, is intended to show people that it is terribly easy to give offence, entirely without meaning to, particularly when individuals are from countries a long way apart on the rope measure. Just because someone forgets to say 'please' when speaking your language, which is foreign to them, does not mean that they are being deliberately rude. On the contrary, they are probably trying very hard to be polite! How hard are you trying to be polite to them?

fact:

People fear the unfamiliar, and that can cause some pretty bad behaviour. We have seen the same member of staff offer both the best and worst of service within the space of a few minutes: a friendly 'Hello, how are you today? Can I give you some help there?' to one customer one minute, a curt 'Yes?' to another the next. The only cause, as far as we could see, was that the two customers he was serving were of different nationalities.

What can you do?: The important thing here is to address the fear. When we were working for a hotel chain in Holland, for example, we found that guests at the main airport hotel were receiving a particularly poor deal in terms of service, and Chinese guests were suffering more than any other. The Dutch hotel staff found them to be so different, they simply didn't know how to deal kindly with them and had given up trying.

Things improved rapidly, however, when we deliberately moved a Chinese employee from another hotel to the airport hotel to look after the Chinese guests. This didn't mean we left her to it on her own; her job was mainly to explain and interpret and mediate and help all parties to understand one another better. It worked fantastically well. Other staff very soon realised that these guests were not aliens from another planet who they couldn't get through to – they were people, just like all the other people they encountered every day, with the same needs. As a result, the staff relaxed, forgot to be afraid, and everyone was much happier.

While you don't want to reinforce any prejudices by pandering to them (allowing white patients to request white nurses in a hospital, for example), there is huge benefit to be gained by maximising the cultural capabilities you have in order to serve your customers in the best possible way.

fact:

If you employ staff from different countries, they will naturally have beliefs, thoughts, behaviours and attitudes towards service that differ widely. As with the supermarket delivery drivers and care home nurses that we talked about above, this can cause fierce clashes between members of staff, which are disruptive and unproductive for everyone.

What can you do?: The cultural dimension *has* to be considered when forming teams. As we said before, some organisations are frightened to address the issue, so frequently it doesn't even get mentioned. What they need to understand though is that talking about these things is not racist (or prejudiced or bigoted or any of the other negatives they fear); it teaches people to *appreciate* difference.

The best way to do this, we've found, is to get all the members of your team to pair up with a colleague of a different nationality and task them with finding out as much as possible about each other's countries. What is the food like? Dress? Climate? What kind of houses do they live in? Do they have gardens? What are their special occasions through the year? What were their schools like? What games did they play as children? What is the thing foreigners find funniest about their countries? You get the picture. Perhaps they could then make little presentations about their discoveries to the rest of the team. Alternatively, ask one member of staff per week to give a short talk about their home country, or maybe hold 'international food' lunches on Fridays, when people take it in turns to bring in things they would eat at home with their families.

It doesn't really matter what form you use to encourage people to find out about each other. The only important thing is that it happens. There is nothing like it for engendering understanding and improving harmony in the workforce!

fact:

If you try to be culturally appropriate to every single customer, you are going to get it wrong, however hard you try. It is simply impossible not to make mistakes. We saw a funny example on the TV a few weeks ago. A British athlete up on a podium in Europe was receiving a medal and a large bouquet of flowers. He obviously knew he was expected to kiss the girl handing them to him, at least once. He managed the first kiss fine and was beginning to straighten up when he realised another was coming; stayed for that, then stood up and waved to the crowd...only to have the girl bump her nose on his chest. She'd gone in for a third, and he wasn't expecting it!

What can you do?: Recognise that no one can learn every detail of every culture, it's impossible. So there are only two things that you and your staff can do.

The first thing is to **smile**! This may sound obvious, but smiling is the *only* thing that is universal across the world and means the same to all people. It is the global indicator of friendliness and goodwill, and all customers will appreciate it, wherever they come from. Kisses, handshakes, bows, waves...all can cause upset of different kinds to different people if they're the wrong sort, so don't even try.

The second thing is to be **interested**. People worry about asking questions. They are afraid this will be seen as being nosy, or they have a tendency to feel that they should know already. This is crazy. How are you ever going to know how to spell Llanfairpwllgwyngyllgogerychwyrndrobwllllantysiliogogogoch – the name of your Welsh customer's home town – if you don't ask? In fact, names are an excellent opportunity. No one will be offended by someone who smiles and says, 'That's an interesting name...where does it come from? You might need to help me spell it!' In fact, you and your Welsh customer may both emerge laughing from the encounter, especially when she tells you that the town name actually means 'The church of St Mary in the hollow of white hazel trees near the rapid whirlpool by St Tysilio's of the red cave'. You've learned something interesting; she's had the chance to tell you a fascinating fact about her home. Your showing interest has encouraged a good response from her. Both of you feel that it has been a good customer experience.

In short, it is not bad service if you don't know what is culturally appropriate for your customer. All you need to do is to show friendly intentions by smiling and showing interest in the customer as a person, and the rest will take care of itself. Give yourself, and your staff, permission to be curious!

key learning points

● Multiculturalism is increasing rapidly. This is great, but it makes for a more complex world and more challenges for service givers.

- Huge increases in travel, off-shoring of call centres, relaxing of borders between countries, globalisation of business and so on makes this an issue that affects **everyone**.
- Businesses put a great deal of effort into being culturally appropriate to every individual they encounter. This is fine if they are dealing mainly with people of one nationality or operating in one particular country, but it doesn't help those offering service to a huge variety of people in quick succession.
- You cannot ignore culture; it is fundamental to who people are. Neither can you expect others to conform to your cultural norms. However it is impossible to learn all the customs and sensitivities of every culture.
- Instead, it is important to recognise the innate judge/dismiss response and actively to *choose* how to behave.
- Open your eyes to the cultural differences within and between your team members *and* between your team and your customers, and find ways to help people discover more about each other.
- Use the cultural capability you have within your team or organisation to serve your customers in the best way.
- Smiling – the international expression of goodwill – and showing interest are the best ways of overcoming cultural difference.
- Be curious – and being curious will be great service itself.

chapter 10
measuring
customer
service

A SHORT STORY TO START

A friend of ours, Denis, is a good trainer who now works for himself. When he was younger he used to work for the internal training department of a large corporate company. After every session he asked the delegates to complete a feedback form. The forms had to be completed anonymously, so he wasn't allowed to read them, then posted off to head office so that his manager could review them and keep track on how his training was going down with staff, and so that figures could be produced of training scores across the company. So far, so good – sort of. His manager never mentioned them or used them in any appraisals and he never saw any figures? Being the mischievous type (as we said he now works for himself, which is fortunate), the first thing he did was to ask the delegates if they minded him reading them: of course they didn't, they assumed he would read them! He then decided to start sending in bogus feedback forms with wild extremes of scores and comments just to see what would happen...and of course what happened? You've guessed it - absolutely nothing! One day he was in head office and went and spoke to the administrator that the copies of the forms got sent to; 'What exactly happened to the forms he sent through every week?'; 'Oh those' she said, 'I file them for a year and then archive them.' 'Does anyone look at them?' he enquired. 'Oh no there are far too many', and she took him to the room where the feedback forms were kept from every training session, from every delegate across the whole company...thousands and thousands...

What's the point of this vignette? Only that it amply illustrates the first rule of measuring or reporting anything at all:

If you're not going to do anything about it once you've measured it, don't measure it in the first place.

It only wastes everyone's time and makes people cross. 'What gets measured gets done' is a phrase frequently bandied about in the business world. But often it isn't true. 'What gets measured gets measured' is more like it. We know of various companies who measure and measure in their efforts to improve, but then sit on the data. In certain hospitals we've worked with, it can take six months before a ward even knows there's been a complaint. It's been received by the hospital, escalated up then down again, entered into a large report, sent sideways in a few different directions and only then, finally, limped into the place it should have been sent to in the first instance. How can anyone improve under these circumstances?

What such organisations should probably do is *less* measuring – and take a long hard look at what they do **first**. How is the data gathered? Who sees it when it comes in? What happens to it then? How is it presented, and to whom? What actions result from it? What checks are in place to ensure that action is taken?

So if you're thinking of introducing mystery shoppers/feedback forms/customer surveys or anything else in an effort to improve your service, stop! You've got a lot of things to think through first.

WHAT TO MEASURE?

Warning issued, however, we would add hastily that of course we think measuring and monitoring are important. In fact they're essential. How can you know what people are thinking and feeling and experiencing if you don't ask?

So first and foremost, you need to decide exactly *what* you're measuring. Obviously, since this is a book about fantastic customer service, you want to understand how good (or not) your customers' experience is – and many companies naturally rush straight to the horse's mouth and start by introducing measures that involve customers. But there are a lot of other elements that contribute to that experience, that lend themselves to measurement in different ways. So rather than bothering customers from the off, we'd recommend a good look at the following:

1. Basics and magic

Yes, we're back to these again. And in general what we'd say is that you *have* to measure your basics; you can *choose* about whether to measure the magic.

Basics on the whole are quite easy to measure. Either something is happening or it isn't. Say one of your basics is 'to answer every phone call within three rings'. Well – are you or aren't you? Tesco has a good example of this kind of measuring, called 'the one in front' scheme. Every 15 minutes a pop-up appears on every till screen for the checkout operator to enter the number of customers in his or her queue. The figures are fed straight back to the floor controller, whose objective it is to ensure that customers never have more than one person waiting in front of them. The controller will then keep opening (or closing) checkouts to maintain the flow. At the same time, Tesco also measures how fast the till operators scan (which is a bit contentious, but we won't worry about that right now), as well as rigorously evaluating all its other basics such as product availability on a continuous basis.

So list your basics (which you've probably done several times already through the course of this book) and then decide on methods you could use to measure each of them. There are lots of suggestions in the 'How?' section of this chapter about ways in which you could do this.

Because of its less tangible nature, magic can be much trickier to measure. However, thinking back to the discussion in Chapter 2, there are different kinds of magic – some of which are much more easily quantifiable than others. Planned magic, for instance, is a doddle. How many pots of crayons/colouring books/sets of stickers have you given out to children in your restaurant in the last month? Has every guest in your hotel been given the tour of its history on the way to their rooms?

Spontaneous magic is a different beast, but even here we'd argue that there are ways of recording the reactions to it which

measuring customer service

149

are more powerful than any set of figures in a spreadsheet. What about making large copies of thank-you letters and displaying them publicly on noticeboards? Or reproducing them on your intranet? Or binding them into a book that's kept somewhere obvious for people to flick through? Used in this kind of fashion, they not only reward the person who provided the magic with public recognition (see Chapter 8), but they spread a feeling of goodwill, acting as mini firelighters for good service from others too. All it takes is a little imagination on your part.

pause for thought...

Here's a fantastic example of an organisation not only measuring rigorously but, more importantly, doing something with the data.

Our colleague Jeremy decided to take a six-month sabbatical from work. Because there was less money coming into the household during that period, he and his wife swapped where they did their household shopping from Sainsbury's to Lidl. To their amazement, only two weeks into the new regime they received a letter from Sainsbury's. 'Dear Mr and Mrs Brown, we are missing you!' it said. Enclosed was a clutch of discount vouchers for things they bought regularly.

They didn't actually change back as it was still cheaper to shop at Lidl. But this remains an astonishing example of customer service generated by measurement.

One thought, though. For some customers, such an action might actually be too spookily 'Big Brother'-ish and frighten them off from your organisation forever. You need to know your customers before you consider introducing measures of this kind. Frightening one or two here and there is OK... you can't please all people all of the time. Frightening more than a certain percentage, however, is bad for business. What about your customers? How much watching do you think they could stand?

2. Training

There is a direct correlation between the experience your customers receive and the amount of training your staff have been given. As we talked about in Chapter 5, anyone who is not a natural service giver can learn fantastic service skills, but only if they receive regular amounts of training and/or coaching. You might teach everyone to smile, stand up, ask customers their names and so on as part of their induction training, but without frequent refreshment these behaviours gradually become corrupted until there is a considerable mismatch between what has been trained and what is delivered. It pays, therefore, to keep a very sharp eye on who has been trained in what and when, and to make sure that regular updates are provided for all.

In fact we'd go so far as to say that measuring and maintaining your staff training is even more important than measuring what your customers think of you. As long as your staff have the right skills that they use in the right way, your customers will already – probably – be satisfied with the service they receive at their hands.

3. *All* links of the service chain

In the same way as staff training affects customer experience, the service staff receive themselves affects their performance. We're back to the service chain again. It needs to be robust in every link, and again we believe that measuring its strength along its whole length is just as important as measuring the end result. This is what many companies never do.

So, how many mistakes have there been in the pay roll this year? How many times has overtime been miscalculated? How many deliveries have been late? Why did that personnel file go missing? How come there were no vegetarian meals in the canteen last Wednesday? You get the picture.

And don't forget managers either. Remember O2 and the way it monitors how much coaching its managers do? You need to be rigorous in your scrutiny of the way managers manage. If things are being missed, make them part of that manager's personal development plan – then after a reasonable length of time check that too, to make sure improvements are being made. *All* links are part of your general service offering, and if you want this to be outstanding, you need to be vigilant internally as well as externally.

HOW TO MEASURE?

There are many different ways of measuring these days. We've gone measurement crazy in fact – you can't blink without being handed a feedback sheet, survey form, online satisfaction questionnaire etc. So we're not going to list every possible option in this section, as there simply isn't room in one book. Instead, we'll look at general types of measurement and how to make them effective, before discussing some interesting ideas to get your juices flowing.

Here are some general types of measurement. The most common (and arguably the most important) is:

Customers measuring you instantly (all feedback, surveys etc.)

By this we mean giving **real** customers the opportunity to rate your service while they're actually receiving it, so that it is instant and genuine. It is the truest and least filtered way of finding out what people think of the experience you offer. Rather than getting customers to fill in yet more forms or tick more boxes, here are some great examples we've seen of ways organisations collect this information:

- In service stations, customers can push either a smiley face button or a grumpy face button on their way out of the toilets, depending on how well maintained they found them.
- Tesco has a 'Fizzback' scheme, inviting customers to text their rating of the service they received as they leave the checkout – all very instant.
- When a customer returns a vehicle to Enterprise Rent-a-Car, they are asked – *every* time, without fail – 'how was the service?', and their reply is noted down in the actual words used. It's slightly different in the US: 'Would you recommend us to a friend?' is the only question customers are asked. Very quick, very effective – there is no better acid test of whether someone approves of your service.
- A while ago, British Airways used to send its staff out among passengers as they waited for their baggage, armed with small ring binders. The staff would ask customers to choose words in the ring binder that best described their experiences of check-in, flight, meals and so on. Again, all very instant. Shame they don't still do it (or at least, they haven't done it to us lately).

Next comes:

Customers measuring you at one remove

Focus groups are the most obvious example of this kind of measurement. They still involve real customers, but at one remove from the experience. As a consequence you gain more of an overview – an opinion not a reaction. This is still very useful as it can be more considered than the instant feedback we've just talked about. It's an ideal means for checking out responses to things such as new products or different store layouts, for example. Tesco's customer forums are massive... they hire a cinema or other large gathering place and invite 300-400 customers in every *week*! If you run a small business, you obviously can't – and don't need to – do anything on this scale, but getting a few people together to see what they think of the pricing on your new line of chocolates, say, can be exceedingly helpful.

Not quite in the same category but related to it is the use of mystery shoppers. It's different because it's a bit artificial, given that mystery shoppers are not actually real customers. However, they do have the advantage of actively noticing the service they receive, which *is* genuine, and can consequently give you an excellent view of what is being offered to your end users.

Lastly we have:

Companies measuring themselves

We've discussed already why this is so important, in terms of ensuring that all links of your service chain are fit for purpose. And there are a myriad of ways in which to do internal measurement.

Tesco, as mentioned previously, uses means like the 'one in front' scheme, but there are many other methods too. Accor, for example, has its staff measuring one another, with a policy whereby members can nominate other colleagues whenever they see them performing particularly well. However, in our opinion you need to be careful with systems such as this. While it is great that people learn to recognise and thereby reinforce positives, there's such a thing as being *too* positive. If your measurement system *only* records the positive, you don't get a balanced picture of what your performance is like overall. So we would suggest that this kind of feedback needs to be offset with a different system that captures a more complete picture.

Quantitative versus qualitative measurement

In the interests of making data collection and analysis easy, many companies opt for the numerical type of measurement. You've seen it a thousand times: 'How would you rate the atmosphere in our restaurant/cleanliness of our trains/gorgeousness of whatever, on a scale of 1 – 5?' asks the little feedback card. So you tick a box somewhere in the middle, and some numbers person in a back office somewhere feeds your rating into a big database that spits out a mighty report at the end of each quarter. So far, so good.

The trouble is, though, that just using numbers in this way has an unfortunate effect: it evens everything out, to become completely uniform every time. Eurostar had this experience. They measured every aspect of the experience they offered to customers, rated on a scale of 1 – 10. But when they looked back at all the results, they found every single one of them was 7-point-something, with no variation. They concluded that this was probably because of people's tendency to rate somewhere in the middle of whatever scale is used – no one ever gives a 9, and no one ever gives a 1. The company had originally believed that actual comments were not important, having offered customers the opportunity to rate them on so many aspects of their service. But without the granularity of comments, the numbers had become meaningless.

There's another important point to make too. Numbers alone are totally unemotional in terms of generating action. The best companies amalgamate numbers with customer stories to improve areas where improvement is needed. They have learned that it is essential to make results 'real' on some human level in order for them to mean anything to people.

This effect can be compared to things like news reports about droughts in Africa or earthquakes in Japan. There are millions of people dying and struggling in either situation, but more fortunate populations elsewhere in the world sit and watch their TVs and feel nothing more than faintly sad. However, should the news report feature one particular child who's suffering from starvation or one weeping man looking through the rubble of his house for his elderly mother, the world sits up and pays attention. Wallets are taken out, rescue teams are sent, governments muster troops to help. The collapse of the San José mine in Chile in 2010 and the eventual rescue of the 33 trapped miners has to be one of the most striking examples of this phenomenon. The entire world held its breath as the men were finally hauled to freedom, and the celebrations were global. People everywhere felt that the men had become personal friends, entirely thanks to the fact that the media had broadcast so much information about them.

While nothing so dramatic is likely to show itself in your customer feedback (hopefully, anyway!) these examples do show the power of the one-off customer story. While you need to be careful that they do not send people careering off on some shoot-from-the-hip reaction, used wisely such stories can be more powerful than anything else in prompting action to improve matters.

The same applies to video, which is particularly effective at helping staff to improve their performance. In call centres, for instance, where 'calls may be recorded for training purposes', there is nothing like sitting down with individuals to watch or listen to either very good or very bad examples of service to communicate the message you want to get across!

Some slightly dangerous means of measurement
Rather than simply recommending that you stick to tried-and-trusted, traditional, established – aka boring – methods of measuring, we're including some examples of measures that we think have added impact, purely because they are more interesting than the norm. Perhaps they may inspire some ideas of your own!

- Pret A Manger arms its mystery shoppers with £50 notes – to be handed out if the shopper encounters really outstanding service from an individual.

- Birmingham Children's Hospital sticks its feedback forms at different heights on the walls, so children can reach them. They also get the kids to draw their experiences, rather than waffle on about them. Brilliant!
- Amazon aims for a measure of zero per cent customer contact. If they never have to speak to a customer in person, they know they're offering fantastic service.
- Carphone Warehouse prints out a list of everyone in the company, with the average score given by customers and colleagues next to each name. They never say a word, but simply stick up a new list every three months. Staff line up to look at it.
- We love the idea of a 'tube-o-meter', that customers can fill with coloured balls depending on how they feel. You can do something like asking them to vote on one area they feel could be improved (out of a choice of five), or which charity they'd like money to go to this month (Waitrose does something similar with big clear boxes of coloured counters). Don't simply give people the choice of yes or no, though, as the result is likely to be skewed. Asking questions like 'Did you enjoy your time with us?' nearly always elicits a 'Yes' answer, even if that wasn't really the case!

TO BE CONSIDERED

So much for the 'what to measure' and the 'how to measure it'. We now also want to talk about a few issues that can arise in the measuring arena that you'll need to watch out for.

Misuse and abuse of measures (fixing)

Where there is a target, there is also inevitably a way of evading/ bending/changing that target in some way – and (almost) always a person ready to do the evading. For example, the NHS has a target of four hours' waiting time in A&E. In other words, if someone brings in their elderly mother who has slipped on the ice and possibly broken her wrist, they shouldn't have to wait for more than four hours before seeing someone about it. The danger is that if A&E is quiet, staff will know those people have only been waiting for an hour – and go off to do something else for three more! Not that this happens in the NHS, of course, ever. So to overcome this manipulation of targets, make sure you have both a maximum target and an incentive to encourage higher performance if possible.

Structuring responses

What questions you ask and how is significant when requesting feedback, so you need to be careful. For example, the schools of two of our colleagues' children recently conducted parent satisfaction surveys. One of the schools issued very structured forms, with headings for different areas of feedback and several multiple choice options where parents could tick things like 'Excellent', 'Satisfactory' or 'Less than Satisfactory'. The other school handed out a more-or-less blank sheet of paper and invited parents to 'write your comments here'. The school with the structured forms received marvellous feedback, with almost universal delight being expressed by parents. The unstructured one attracted a whole heap of moaning.

Now this could be because the first school was fab and the second was dreadful, but going by Ofsted reports and other official measures, this seems unlikely. In our experience, it was simply that offering an unstructured free-for-all way of giving feedback virtually encourages people to whine. They think they have to say something, even when they felt perfectly happy at the outset – and 'something' usually means 'something negative'.

It can also be argued, of course, that the unstructured approach leaves people free to express their real feelings, and that therefore you gain a truer picture of the actual situation. Either way, it needs thinking about...you don't simply want to give people a chance to bash you, do you?

Doing something about it

We're sorry to go on about it, but we're going to say it again. When you've got the data, you need to do something about it. More than this, you need to do something about it *now*. We've heard the slogan 'fixing for the future' being bandied about in the health service of late. What? The future's the future: how about the person shouting at you right this minute? Wherever possible, you need to be able to sort things out immediately – and so few organisations do it. In hotels, for instance, you're often asked 'how was your stay?' as you check out. Even if you say 'awful' (as we have on a few occasions, just to see what happens), you'll invariably receive the response, 'oh, I'm so sorry. Ah well, here's your bill anyway'!

Why can't everyone be like the US-based Promise Hotels? If you're not happy with your stay, they'll tear your bill up – while asking the reason for your unhappiness. Say you said it was because the shower didn't work. They'll then go to the department responsible for showers, and *they'll* pay your bill instead. Genius! Not only are you delighted with Promise, but the shower department will be a lot more careful in future. Two birds killed with one stone.

Virgin too is very good at fixing now. If the meal you wanted on the plane is not available or you had to move seats or some other minor disaster occurred, a smiling steward will turn up with a bottle of champagne in recompense. Fantastic! As a customer, you almost *hope* something will go wrong. That's a point which every business should be trying to reach. What about you?

key learning points

- Please, don't measure for the sake of measuring. Unless you mean to do something with the data you collect, you'll only waste everyone's time and annoy people.

- That said, measuring is vital – or you'll never know what customers are really experiencing at your hands. And if you don't know this, you can't possibly hope to be fantastic at it.

- Measuring your basics is essential. Magic is trickier, but you can still do it if you are imaginative in how you go about it. Knowledge being power, we'd advise you to monitor everything that can possibly be monitored.

- Measuring what goes into creating your customer experience is equally important as measuring the experience itself. Consequently, you need to be rigorous about assessing what training your staff have received and when, as well as how every link in your service chain is performing – on a regular basis.

- There are infinite ways to evaluate. Choosing to be interesting in how you do it, however, can be more effective and powerful than always opting for more traditional methods.

- There are three main areas you need information on: what customers think of you in the moment they experience your service; what they think of you when they've had time to consider; and how your own organisation rates what it does.

- Numbers are important tools – but they need to be translated into real human experience before they can become true engines of change. If you want to improve what you do, you need to come up with ways of engaging people's emotions so that they'll *want* to improve.

- Beware of setting targets that are easily manipulated, and of those who like to manipulate them for their own convenience.

- And again, please note, do *not* measure for the sake of measuring. Do something with the data you collect, and preferably do it now!

chapter 11
Pulling it all together

Here we are, on the last chapter. You've read it all now: we've taken you through tools, ideas, principles, examples both good and bad, exercises, best and worst practice and more. You've thought about what your brand is, what you're trying to achieve, how to attract the different kinds of loyalty, what issues you might need to address. You've heard our recommendations on how to lead for customer service and how to create service leaders and managers; how to create the perfect service environment through signals; how to train and reward your staff; whether the cultural mix in your organisation is creating issues with customers – and so on and so forth.

In fact, you're probably now suffering from information overload and wondering what you're meant to *do* with all this? Where do you start?

GET TO THE HEART OF THE MATTER

The first thing to say is that no company won't have done something about the things we have discussed throughout this book. There will certainly be some element of service training or measurement of satisfaction or means to understand customers better in place already. The second thing is that whatever you do will never be complete: improving service is not a specific, finite piece of work, it's an ongoing process. So, a) you will not be starting from scratch, and b) this won't be one project with a certain end, it will be more about creating a constant awareness with various activities that shift around you at different times.

So the place to begin is to gain a proper understanding of where you've already got to. And when we say proper, we mean proper. It is no use reading reports or studying statistics, you really need to get in there and experience it for yourself – from three different perspectives: your customers, your staff and your managers/team leaders. In other words, you need to understand what it is like to be any one of the links in your service chain.

Pulling it all together

163

Without a true picture of circumstances as they are now, you can't understand your starting point.

Here are two perfect examples of why this is so important.

case studies

THE HOTEL

At one of the big hotel chains, head office required all guest numbers and other figures in from each hotel by Friday lunchtime, in order to gain a consolidated view of the week just past and to plan for the week to come. Accordingly, the finance people would begin phoning around the hotels from the time they got in on the Friday morning at 8.30 a.m. They couldn't understand why, frequently, the hotel managers didn't answer their phones or, if they did, were brusque and unforthcoming, or fobbed them off altogether. This became a real problem – a 'them and us' situation between head office and the hotels. It was only when we went and asked the hotel managers why this was such an issue that we discovered the root of the problem. Friday mornings, before about 9.30 a.m., are the busiest time of the week for hotels, with massive numbers of week-time guests checking out, change-over cleans taking place, accounts being settled, new bookings being taken, cars fetched, suitcases carried and so on. The last thing managers needed at that time was the finance department on the phone wanting the fine detail of the week's business! So we checked with Finance. What time did they actually need the figures in by? Would it be OK to wait until 10 a.m. before phoning? Yes? Excellent! And that was the end of the problem. Finance knew in theory that Fridays were busy for the hotels, but hadn't appreciated what that meant in practice.

THE HOSPITAL

For most hospitals, the most important issue, above just about any other, is infection control. And just one measure that many adopt is not to allow nurses to arrive in uniform – they have to change once they get to work. This is very sensible. But in one hospital we worked with, we discovered that there wasn't anywhere for the nurses to get changed, except in the toilets. And where is the principal source of germs and bacteria in any building? Yes, you've got it in one.

The point of both these examples is the whole experience thing. Neither is obvious unless you are actually there, working alongside the staff involved, when suddenly, bang...the problems are there glaring you in the face – and actually, so are the solutions. It's a bit like 'The Secret Millionaire'. The participants know about poverty or knife crime or teenage pregnancy or whatever, but suddenly when they're there experiencing these things for themselves by living among them, it's an absolute revelation to them – and often a life-changing one. Really getting to the heart of matters is also the best route for anyone looking to make truly company-changing improvements!

THE BEST WAY IN

So what's the best way to get into your customer's shoe like this? Going undercover seems to be a popular trend at the moment, with a proliferation of TV programmes like 'Undercover Boss' etc., and it's true that this would probably gain you the most complete picture of what it's really like to be one of your customers or one of your delivery drivers, or whoever. Certainly, many companies use elements of it to understand their customers' experience – employing mystery shoppers, for example – and we often get our clients to phone up their own organisations, as customers, to make enquiries, which is a very useful exercise. But cloak and dagger stuff is not always practical – and in our opinion, it's not actually necessary.

The important thing to do is to identify each link in your service chain and then to spend time, a few days probably, working alongside the people within those links. It might be a bit awkward for the first hour or so, everyone feeling all self-conscious (which is why just visiting doesn't work), but this wears off in no time and a true picture emerges of the challenges being faced by those people.

WHAT DO YOU WANT?

With this kind of insight gained, you can then start to formalise what it is you want to achieve – either overall, or within a specific area. We've been doing some work with Parkland, for example, an oil retailer in Canada which sells on petrol to filling stations. In their business, operational efficiency is the most important thing – a smooth, cost-effective transition between themselves and the garages is what makes them good at what they do. So their service all needs to be geared towards creating this efficiency. They don't need to worry so much about fostering a warm, welcoming manner towards customers; they *do* need to make sure the logistics part of their service works like greased lightning. In other words, it's all about what you want to achieve, as this will affect the type of service you need to provide. Service is a means to an end. What is your end?

SEEING A VISION

With the objective identified, you can then see the gap between where you are and where you want to get to, and decisions can be made about how to bridge it. Often this means establishing a project in one particular area. Just as with any business project, you can establish a business case to justify your proposed change, identify who the stakeholders will be, draw up a project plan and so on. There's just one note of caution we'd like to sound about this approach though: because service is all about people, you need to make sure the personal touch doesn't get swallowed in project process. The focus needs to remain on the customer at all times, whether the customer in question is the person who buys your end product or the person who stacks your shelves. There is no point building a beautiful new ward without asking the nurses who work there about the best layout or most practical taps to put on the sinks.

When we're working with clients, what we often do is to create a vision – to paint a picture of what this planned improvement will be like – and to make it as real and detailed as possible. What will people be doing/saying/hearing/feeling about this improvement? What will it smell like? What will it feel like? What will it sound like? Mercure, for instance, wanted to improve the experience in its hotel bars. Great! But what should the bars look like? Fun local pubs with live music? Swish city bars with coloured neon lights? Quiet, conservative country clubs? What?

exercise

PAINTING YOUR VISION EXERCISE

The great thing about creating a vision is that you can (and should) get everyone involved in establishing what it should be. Not only do you get a better, more detailed vision, but you gain everyone's buy-in to the improvement when it happens. Here's a great exercise that you can do with any number of staff, to get their creative juices flowing and generate an energy and excitement about changes you're thinking of making.

Working with a small group of staff, give them all a small canvas (or A3 card) and some paints, ask them to paint a simple picture or image of what they would like the vision of service to be like. Once they have completed their picture ask them to hand their picture to the colleague next to them; their colleague then adds to the vision they have just been handed. This is repeated ideally for a few rounds or until the picture comes around to the originator. Ask them to describe what they see and to then start capturing the words they use to describe a collective vision of service. These words and these images then become the start of the service vision.

PRIORITISING AND DEVELOPING MOMENTUM

Once you've done all this, you can start bringing together the pieces of the jigsaw required to fill the gaps you've found. Anything good that you're already doing, transfer across, then add in new elements that support and develop them.

However, even when you've identified your issues and spotted the gaps, you may still feel unsure of priorities. Should you start with head office, or is a training scheme for your customer-facing staff more important? If the latter, should you be looking at establishing how staff interact with customers, or at developing a new set of behaviours? Or maybe it's most important to work with your managers and team leaders, as one of the key things in service is how staff are managed. After all, happier staff make for better customer experience, as night follows day.

Obviously we can't be prescriptive here, as every business is different. However what we would advise is to start where you can get going most easily. A frequent retailer choice, for example, is to start with the environment – to pilot a new design of store, say. This tends to be a good one, as there is often a significant boost to the business when new store designs go out.

The trick, though, is then not to finish where you can most easily.

> Start where you can start most easily, but do not then finish where you can finish most easily!

Say for example all your restaurants are already in the process of being spruced up. What you need to do then is to think, 'Great, now we've boosted our environment. *What's next?* Accor is really good at this. Whenever they open a new hotel or refurbish an old one, they instigate a whole suite of extra staff training in that hotel, regardless of how long someone might have worked for them or how experienced they might be. Frequently, clients ask us to start with staff – providing training or implementing a regular coaching system or similar. And of course we do this. But then we move on to the next logical area for improvement, whether this be adding new skills for managers and team leaders or finding a way of sustaining staff enthusiasm, such as implementing a rewards scheme.

In other words, once you have started it is essential to gain and maintain momentum. Keep on pushing and continuously adding all the elements we've talked about throughout this book, in whichever order seems most practical. All the tools you'll need are right here in your hands. If you've decided that your starting point is your service environment, go back and re-read 'Signals of Service' and 'Training Your Customer'. If training staff is your first priority, 'Creating Service Heroes' and 'Service Across Cultures' are there to help. If it's management, 'Managing for Great Service', 'Rewards and Recognition' and 'Measuring Service' will all come in useful. Good luck!

ONE MORE THING

Of the many wise things Mahatma Gandhi said during his life, 'be the change you want to see in the world' is the most apposite quotation for our next point. Remember what we said about making sure the personal didn't get lost in the process when instigating service improvement projects? One good way of ensuring this doesn't happen is to make your improvement project mirror the customer experience. You need to reflect the style of what you want to achieve in the way that you achieve it. If you want your new restaurant to be fun, chatty, lively and energetic, for example, the project to create it needs to be equally fun, chatty, lively and energetic – or more so. Or if you want the atmosphere in your health shop to be gentle, refreshing and professional, the project to make it so has to be 'it' too...and the leader of the project has to be 'it plus'. In this way, you can both make the change genuine right from the start and also create a precedent for how it continues. Be the change you want to see...

AND FINALLY

If you should happen to be reading this and thinking, 'Hold on, this is all very well for a big gun in a large corporate; I can't possibly change the whole organisation/I'm just a small business owner/ team leader etc., this can't apply to me' – stop right there! Yes, it does apply to you – in exactly the same way. Think about what you want to achieve; to sell more sweets in your small shop? To make your service more personal in your wedding business? Just as for big businesses, you need to: become your customer again (or your staff member); identify the gaps between where you are and where you want to get to; create a vision; start where you can start. And then off you go. This process doesn't just work for corporates, it's for anyone who provides any kind of customer experience!

JUST ONE LAST WORD

A great deal of this book has been about your organisation, whatever size it may be – thinking about your staff, your customers, your market, your environment, your everything else.

But what about you? Think carefully about yourself. Here you are reading this book, saying 'I think I need to improve my customer experience' and 'Right, let's do it' and other positive, gung-ho things. So, should it be you who leads this? Are you the right person to create/develop/train/design/implement it? Remember the head of the hotel chain, who loved financials but didn't really 'do' service? Are you a 50-year-old manager in a youth clothes shop like Superdry – and if so, do you really 'get' what's required? You need to be honest here. It doesn't actually matter whether you're the right person or not. All that does matter is that you understand the need for change, identify what form it should take and then appoint the right leader, whether that's you or not.

key learning points

- You can't start to improve your whole customer experience – or even discover if it needs improving – without understanding exactly where you are already. And you can't understand that properly from reading reports or studying statistics. You need to experience this for yourself – really experience it – by rolling up your sleeves and getting stuck in, working alongside the people at the coalface.
- Your understanding needs to be from three different perspectives: those of your customers, your manager/team leaders, and your staff.
- When you've identified the issues, you can work out what you want to achieve – and see the real difference between where you are now and where you want to get to.
- Creating a vision, and involving other people in doing this, is a great way to start moving towards your ultimate goal. It generates enthusiasm and motivation.
- It doesn't really matter where you start with your improvements – in fact it's usually best simply to start with

what is easiest. The trick is then not to stop again, but to keep moving forward and tackling one area at a time. This book has all the tools you need!

- Make the change process mirror what you're trying to achieve. If your goal is cool and funky, have a cool and funky project to achieve it.
- If you need a cool and funky project but you are not a cool and funky person yourself, think very carefully about whether you are the right person to lead it!

index